FAITHFUL LEADERSHIP

Learning to Lead With Power

Thomas R. Hawkins

D1056636

DISCIPLESHIP RESOURCES

P.O. BOX 840 • NASHVILLE, TENNESSEE 37202-0840

www.discipleshipresources.org

To Ruth Marie Hawkins,

who understands how the power to serve nurtures growth

Cover and book design by Sharon Anderson and Lori Haley

ISBN 0-88177-253-4

Library of Congress Catalog Card No. 98-86151

DR253

Contents

Introduction

Servanthood & the Absence of Leadership

The Bible reminds us that we usually experience the mystery of God's presence in the midst of absence. As Israel wandered in the desert wilderness, a cloud on the horizon or a gust of wind hinted at God's guiding presence. Elijah encountered God not in the storm and earthquake but in the sound of sheer silence and absence (1 Kings 19:12). Isaiah proclaimed that God's presence manifests itself in what appears as absence (Isaiah 45:15). After his ascension, Jesus' physical absence allowed him to be spiritually present among his followers in a new, empowering way. Jesus' physical absence set the stage for the Holy Spirit's descent at Pentecost.

God's absence can be felt in many ways. Some people experience an absence of leadership in the church as an absence of God's power, presence, and purpose. Yet it is possible that this very absence mysteriously discloses new possibilities for divine presence.

In some communities, an empty parsonage symbolizes this absence. In other situations, empty pews convey a sense of abandonment and absence. Still elsewhere, the committee on nominations and personnel submits a mostly empty slate of officers and church leaders to the charge conference. Even worse, the committee submits a full report only to satisfy the district superintendent's need for a complete set of mailing addresses, knowing that many people on this report will never serve. In some congregations, bitter conflict among church leaders results in a painful absence of spiritual communion. This absence is not limited to local congregations and denominational structures. Laity and clergy puzzle over the strange silence of the church in the public square. The church's moral leadership seems absent from public discourse in an increasingly secular culture.

We usually bemoan these experiences of absence. We praise earlier times when great leaders guided our congregations and directed our denomination. If we could only return to these former times and more traditional models of leadership, then all would be well. Unfortunately, this response may cause us to overlook a new experience of divine presence hidden in, with, and under the apparent absence of leadership in the church. Perhaps our experiences of absence are inviting us to discover new forms of leadership through which God empowers and enlivens our ministries.

JESUS' ABSENCE AS AN EMPOWERING PRESENCE

In the garden, the risen Jesus asks Mary not to cling to his physical presence and tells her to return to the community. She goes back to the other disciples and bears witness to Jesus' resurrection (John 20:18). Mary is not dependent, clinging, and mesmerized by a powerful leader. She does not cling to Jesus' physical presence. She instead embraces his absence and discovers a new form of spiritual presence. This expression of divine presence emerges out of absence. It empowers Mary to lead, to bear witness to the Resurrection, and to continue Jesus' own ministry of proclamation and service.

Jesus' disciples later have the same experience at the Ascension. Jesus physically leaves his disciples when he ascends to heaven. He will no longer stand among them as their leader. In the midst of this absence, the disciples discover new and unanticipated resources for leading the emerging church.

The disciples are standing on Mount Olivet, looking up to the heavens where Jesus has just ascended. The angels appear and ask, "Men of Galilee, why do you stand looking up toward heaven?" (Acts 1:11). When the disciples return to Jerusalem and are gathered together in the upper room, they suddenly experience an outpouring of the Holy Spirit. This experience empowers them for mission and witness. They are not to look up to an authority figure who can tell them what to do. They discover, in the midst of absence, an unsuspected divine presence that bestows the power to lead in ways they never dreamed possible. In the absence of Jesus' physical leadership, a new power to lead emerges among the disciples.

Like the disciples, we honor Jesus' absence when, as Christian communities, we do not look for a single leader to ride into town on a white horse and save us. We honor Jesus' absence when we do not "look up" to a single human leader on whom we can depend for everything. We honor Jesus' absence when we discover the Spirit of Jesus the Servant animating us as a Christian community of faith.

LEADING WITH POWER-OVER, POWER-WITH, AND POWER-WITHIN

We can discern three different ways in which the apostles lead with power as they discover God's presence amid the absence of Jesus' physical leadership: *power-over*, *power-with*, and *power-within*.[1]

LEADING WITH *POWER-OVER*

In Jesus' absence, some of the early apostles lead with *power-over*. This power derives from their official positions and offices in the emerging church—we call it positional power. Clearly, Peter plays this role in Acts. As the one whom Jesus called the rock upon which he will establish his church, Peter provides direction. He orients the apostles to their roles and tasks. He reminds them of the values, behaviors, and norms established by Jesus when he taught them. Yet he does not exercise this power to lead in authoritarian or dominating ways. He places his *power-over* at the service of the community. He acts as a servant to the assembly. He does not make decisions about Judas' replacement arbitrarily and autonomously. Rather, he uses his positional power to mediate power and authority to the community (Acts 1:15-26). In the absence of Jesus' former leadership, Peter discovers new resources for leading with power. A mysterious new divine presence is hidden beneath an apparent absence of Jesus' direct leadership.

Later, the early church refuses to keep positional power centralized in a few offices. The apostles do not cling to power. They resist the temptation to be heroic leaders who can do everything themselves. They instead create new structures of authority that give away their power to others. They establish a diaconate to care for those in need. Significantly, the apostles draw upon their memory of Jesus the Servant in naming this office. These new leaders are called deacons. *Diakonos* cannot be misunderstood as an honorific description. It allows no room for domination. The Greek word refers to the humble activity of serving tables. Positional power and authority are meant for service, not subordination.

LEADING WITH *POWER-WITH*

The whole community experiences a second form of power on Pentecost. As the Spirit descends upon them with rush of wind and tongues of fire, they go forth to lead with *power-with* (Acts 2:1-4). Power—including *power-with*—emerges from relationships within community. It is not a personal possession. It is not a power packet that an individual owns. It is a dynamic force that flows from community and relationship.

Power-with does not seek warm intimacy and a close fellowship. Its objective is to continue the ministry of service to the world begun in Jesus' own ministry. The apostles gathered in the upper room do not lock the doors and enjoy their experience of *power-with*. They fling wide the doors and go into the streets, preaching to pilgrims from around the world who have gathered in Jerusalem. They use their *power-with* to serve God's mission of redemption and reconciliation. Jesus has already begun this project, and it now continues—in his absence—through his followers. The purpose of *power-with* is not warm fellowship among the like-minded. The purpose is to advance the ministry of Jesus the Servant, who taught, healed, included the outcast, and invited the marginalized to God's banquet table.

The early Christian community holds everything in common, spends much time together in prayer, and shares in common meals (Acts 2:44-46). Yet these experiences of *power-with* do not close them off to the world beyond them. The early church does not over-focus on members and their own needs. The apostles instead reach out through acts of inclusion and hospitality. Service to strangers becomes a catalyst for new partnerships in the gospel (Acts 2:47).

LEADING WITH *POWER-WITHIN*

According to the Book of Acts, the apostles also lead with a third type of power: *power-within*. They have charismatic gifts of healing and preaching. Peter and John heal the lame beggar at the Beautiful Gate (Acts 3:1-10). People carry the sick into the streets so that Peter's shadow can fall upon them (Acts 5:15). The apostles possess special expertise that developed from their personal knowledge of Jesus and his ministry (Acts 3:11-26). Yet they do not employ their power to lead in order to bedazzle and mesmerize. They do not insist on being the center of attention. Instead, they "de-center" themselves. They become servants to others, giving away their power. They lay hands on others, sharing their power and incorporating the others into the church's mission and witness.

When the early church scatters following Stephen's martyrdom, Philip flees Jerusalem and preaches in Samaria. While ministering in Samaria, Philip encounters Simon. According to the Book of Acts, Simon practices magic, amazing the Samaritans and telling them that he is someone great. The Samaritans even say that Simon himself represents "the power of God that is called Great" (8:10). Simon is a perfect example of the dark side of *power-within*. Simon uses his charismatic gifts to bedazzle and to make himself the center of attention. Rather than strengthen people, Simon makes them dependent upon him. He then exploits these dependencies for his own benefit.

When Simon tries to buy God's power with money, Peter rebukes him, "May your silver perish with you, because you thought you could obtain God's gift with money!" (Acts 8:20). Unlike Simon, Philip puts his *power-within* at the service of God's divine project and the needs of others. The power of service eclipses the power of bedazzlement.

SERVANT LEADERSHIP AS PRESENCE AMID ABSENCE

All three ways of leading with power—*power-over, power-with*, and *power-within*—can be wielded in ways that give life or deal death. *Power-over* can either dominate or empower. *Power-with* can turn in upon itself, leading to a closed fellowship, or it can reach out to others in acts of service and inclusion. *Power-within* can be used to mesmerize and bedazzle or to augment people's strength. In each case, the difference between the two outcomes is *servanthood*.

In many of Jesus' parables, servants are left in charge in the master's absence. A man who was going on a journey entrusted his property to his servants (Matthew 25:14-30; Luke 19:11-27). A man built a vineyard, leased it to tenants, and then sent servants to administer it (Mark 12:1-12; Luke 20:9-19).

Servants exercise leadership in the master's absence. They are called to act reliably and faithfully. The absent master depends upon their service. Paul describes early church leadership in these terms: "Think of us in this way, as servants of Christ and stewards of God's mysteries" (1 Corinthians 4:1). Leadership in the early church occurs in the absence of Christ, who will eventually come and judge the people's work. "Therefore do not pronounce judgment before the time, before the Lord comes, who will bring to light the things now hidden in darkness and will disclose the purposes of the heart" (4:5). In our own experience of the absence of leadership in the church, perhaps we will discover a new and surprising divine presence as our servanthood guides and shapes how we lead with power.

When leaders understand themselves as servants who exercise power in the master's absence, they are less likely to employ their *power-over* in ways that dominate. They instead perceive differences in positional power as temporary conditions that can ultimately evolve into relationships of mutuality and equality. Servanthood reminds leaders that their task is to strengthen everyone's capacity to serve in the master's absence, not to make others dependent upon the leaders' willingness and gift-edness for service. *Power-within* is thus purged of its tendency to bedazzle, mesmerize, and insist on being the center of atten-tion. When leaders recall that they are servants who continue the master's ministry of witness, healing, and proclamation in Jesus' absence, they are less inclined to allow *power-with* to degenerate into an inwardly focused exclusivism that ignores the world's hurts and needs.

QUESTIONS FOR REFLECTION

1. Can you give some examples of how we experience an absence of leadership in the contemporary church? Where do you see an absence of leadership?

2. The chapter proposes a paradox: Even in the midst of absence we can experience a mysterious divine presence. Describe some situations in which you believe that God was present or hidden in the midst of what felt like absence?

3. In the biblical world, servants exercised leadership in the master's absence. How is servanthood a good metaphor for leadership in today's church or world? What are its strengths? What are its weaknesses or liabilities as an image of leader-ship?

Leading With Power

A CRISIS IN LEADERSHIP

What does it mean to lead with power? Leaders play a crucial role in building vital congregations, yet more frequently than not we experience an absence of leaders and leadership. Many church members are passive and withdrawn. A small minority lead maintenance ministries. Still fewer leaders actively engage in ministries of outreach, caring, and mission. The fields are ripe for harvest, and the need for leaders is painfully obvious. Why, then, do churches experience an absence of leaders? In many cases, traditional leader behaviors may themselves be at fault.

SOME LEADERS OFTEN MODEL STATUS AND PRIVILEGE RATHER THAN SERVICE

Church members sometimes look at how their leaders behave and say, "If this is what it means to be a church leader, I want nothing to do with it." Some church leaders expect to be served and obeyed. They see themselves as elected to run the church rather than to find ways that members themselves can make decisions about their common life. Other church leaders claim special privilege and status. They assume that they can make claims on other people's time and resources simply because they hold a church office. They thus communicate that leading is about status and privilege rather than service and mutuality. Those who value partnership and collaboration have no interest in becoming leaders when such behaviors typify church life.

The coordinator of the spring banquet, for example, becomes enraged because he does not have a prominent seat at the head table. The chairperson of the trustees is upset because she was not personally consulted before the church office allowed an outside group to use the fellowship hall. Church members who value service and partnership cannot see themselves as leaders when their present leaders model status, privilege, and entitlement.

Even worse, many church members have encountered leaders who control, manipulate, and coerce. The chairperson deliberately calls a committee meeting on a night when her chief opponent cannot attend, thus excluding him from a crucial vote. Another chairperson belittles committee members' opinions. "If you had been around here as long as I have, you would know that that idea will never work in this congregation," he says.

Church members consequently opt out of leadership. Those who value inclusion, participation, and mutuality find little encouragement to become church leaders. They invest their time, talent, creativity, and imagination in other organizations or activities.

SOME LEADERS MODEL CELEBRITY RATHER THAN SERVICE

Our media-driven American culture poses yet another challenge for leaders. Our culture transforms leaders into celebrities. We become an audience expecting to be entertained and bedazzled rather than a community of people engaged with our leaders in addressing issues. We over-focus on the leader's personality. We consequently undervalue our own roles and responsibilities. Then, when we cease being entertained, we boo the performance off the stage.

Individuals who do not enjoy being the center of attention, who do not crave the glaring footlights of public view, who want to be servants and not celebrities, have difficulty imagining themselves as church leaders.

SOME LEADERS MAKE FRIENDS RATHER THAN MAKE MINISTRY

Some church members are frustrated with the cozy familiarity, the comfortable insider relationships, that develop among leaders. The ultimate goal appears to be fellowship and friendship rather than service and witness. Making ministry happen seems less important than building friendships and supporting other like-minded individuals.

Too often church members see their leaders bogged down in relationships and meetings. They perceive that leadership involves an endless round of meetings. Leadership is about interpersonal intimacy, they conclude. These church members prefer to invest their time and energy in concrete projects where they can make a difference.

CAN WE ENVISION ANOTHER TYPE OF LEADER?

We also have an occasional glimpse into another vision of leadership that excites and inspires. A flow develops between leaders and their constituents. Dreams are shared. Resources are mobilized. Significant goals are accomplished. We look back and exclaim, "God's Spirit was surely moving among us. How else could we have achieved all this?" We delight that the hungry are fed, that children learn the Bible, that youth know the support of a loving community. We feel deep satisfaction that the homeless have shelter, that music has touched worshipers' hearts, that lives are changed.

We also know that some of life's most important friendships develop as leaders work side-by-side with one another. Leading can be life-changing. As we lead, we grow as individuals. We gain an understanding of and an appreciation for people who are different from ourselves. We see ourselves in new ways as we interact with others, thus launching us on journeys of self-discovery. We celebrate gifts we never knew we possessed. We develop new ways to connect faith to life, to link our faith with faithfulness.

All of us struggle to make sense of what it means to lead with power in our congregations and church organizations. After all, we feel ourselves participating in something rich with potential and deeply satisfying. Yet we also find ourselves mired down in frustration and pain.

Sylvia Canivez, Norma Knight, Mike Scott, Howard Parker, and Leon Henry all illustrate different ways we may lead with power.

THREE EXPERIENCES OF POWER

CHARISMA AND CONFLICT

"Norma said that she will not be coming to the United Methodist Women meetings anymore," said Martha Fortney, the UMW's vice president. Pastor Sylvia Canivez was surprised and disturbed. Seventy-year-old Norma Knight had long been the mainstay of Faith Church's UMW unit. In fact, she was Faith Church's most prominent matriarch.

Norma had grown up in Faith Church, in Warrensville, along with her two brothers. When all three of them felt called to ministry in the 1940's, Norma went to the nearby theological seminary along with her brothers. Norma persisted in her theological education despite resistance from seminary professors who clearly did not want a woman in their classes.

Norma's brothers went on to highly successful and visible careers. One brother became a well-known seminary professor. The second brother served large, prominent congregations. He became well known throughout the region as a popular preacher and effective pastor. Norma, shortly before her graduation, married one of her fellow students. Just a few years later, her husband was killed in an auto accident. A grieving Norma returned to Warrensville and Faith Church. Once home, she never left again.

Since her return nearly fifty years ago, Norma had thrown her boundless energy and extensive talents into Faith Church's ministries. Pastors came and went. Norma was always there. She organized study groups, prayed with people, and held things together. Everyone saw Norma as Faith Church's de facto pastor. Periodic visits by her famous brothers only enhanced and solidified her already considerable charismatic authority.

Norma's reputation ultimately extended well beyond Faith Church. The whole community of Warrensville knew her. Regardless of their church affiliation, parents of terminally ill children brought them to Norma for the laying on of hands and prayer. Unchurched couples experiencing marital problems came to her for advice and counsel. Over the years Norma came to symbolize God's power and presence to many people in the community. Her annual leadership in Warrensville's lay-led community Easter sunrise service symbolized her status both in the community and in Faith Church.

When the bishop appointed Sylvia Canivez as Faith Church's first female pastor, Sylvia and Norma immediately formed a close friendship. Sylvia was still confronting some of the same prejudices against women in ministry that Norma had experienced earlier in the century. Sylvia and Norma spent much time together. Their conversations forged a strong bond between the two women. As a result, Norma frequently used her role as church matriarch to advance Sylvia's ideas and projects. When Sylvia introduced inclusive language into worship, Norma's enthusiastic support defused opposition. With little more than a nod of her head during a crucial administrative council meeting, all opposition to Sylvia's plans for a church-based daycare center disappeared.

Even without Norma's support, Sylvia probably would have succeeded. She possessed considerable interpersonal skills and a winsome personality. Sylvia was also an excellent preacher and pastor. She possessed some of the same charisma and personal magnetism that had elevated Norma into her role as church matriarch. Members soon developed a deep appreciation for Sylvia both as a person and as their pastor.

When Sylvia suggested major changes in the church's confirmation program, however, Norma seemed cool and reserved. The source of Norma's discomfort was a mystery to Sylvia. Sylvia believed passionately that confirmation should be changed and modernized. As a former public school teacher, she had concentrated on religious education as a seminary student. In her efforts to convince Faith Church that her opinions about confirmation were correct, Sylvia frequently reminded everyone of her special expertise in education.

During a particularly tense administrative council meeting, a slim majority of members voted in favor of Sylvia's proposed changes. Norma was obviously upset at the outcome and left the meeting without speaking to Sylvia or the council members.

After this meeting, Norma was visibly absent from key church events. She did not come to Faith Church's annual spring bazaar, an event she had initiated decades ago. She also missed the next two administrative council meetings. Sylvia, sensing that Norma's feelings might be bruised, made an appointment to visit with her. During the conversation, Norma was polite but reserved. Neither woman was ready to resolve the unspoken rift between them. When Sylvia heard that Norma had resigned as UMW president, she knew that this resignation was only the first move in a more open conflict between them.

Faith Church's members immediately noticed Norma's abrupt withdrawal from church activities. While no one spoke about it directly to Sylvia, she could hear members whispering about the rift between these two powerful women. Gradually, many groups that had traditionally depended upon Norma's leadership foundered. For a time it appeared that the UMW might actually collapse and disband.

Then Norma suddenly announced to her friends that she was moving to Florida, where her two brothers had already retired. A rousing farewell celebration for Norma gave church members an opportunity to acknowledge her ministry and to bring the relationship to some closure. Sylvia spoke briefly to Norma at the reception, but this superficial encounter left no space for healing. Ultimately, both women moved on in their lives and ministries. Sylvia was relieved, yet she remained disappointed that they had not healed the rift between them. It remained unfinished business for both women.

WHO'S IN CHARGE HERE?

Mike Scott was excited about his new appointment. The district superintendent had just informed him that he would become North Ridge Church's associate pastor as of September 1. Mike already knew North Ridge's senior pastor, Howard Parker. He had served with him on district and conference committees. More important, Howard Parker had been his father's seminary roommate. Mike's father and Howard had remained close friends over the years. Howard had been in and out of Mike's home as long as Mike could remember. Mike viewed Howard almost as a second father. The appointment seemed a perfect match not only to Mike and Howard but also to the bishop and cabinet.

The previous associate had left several months prior to Mike's arrival, so a number of programs had lost momentum. Howard gave Mike complete responsibility for these programs. Mike quickly threw himself into reorganizing the youth ministry and education programs. His efforts immediately produced results.

Howard proudly announced from the pulpit his enthusiasm for Mike's ministry as programs flourished and attendance soared. Yet Mike gradually found Howard's behavior to be somewhat enigmatic. Howard was more distant and reserved than Mike remembered him being. Howard met with Mike and the rest of North Ridge's lay staff every Monday morning. He always asked Mike for an update on issues and projects during these meetings, yet he seldom provided Mike with feedback and appeared to have only a passing interest in what Mike actually did. As long as things went well, Howard seemed rather indifferent to Mike's plans. What would happen, Mike sometimes wondered, if one of his programs failed or caused controversy?

At the end of Mike's first year, church school attendance was still rising and the youth fellowships continued to grow. Mike felt supported by parents and church members, but he increasingly felt that his relationship with Howard was subtly changing. Howard was never openly critical, but he was also never supportive. The Monday-morning staff meetings continued as usual. Howard sometimes made comments or asked questions that suggested that he was uncomfortable with the directions in which Mike was moving. Mike wondered if Howard did not approve of the way Mike managed the youth fellowships and their programs. Howard had a more traditional top-down approach to church programming. Mike, on the other hand, tended to let groups decide upon their own priorities.

Midway through Mike's second year, he led a senior high study on the Christian's responsibility for the environment. At the conclusion of the study, Mike challenged the senior high youth to take concrete steps to care for the environment. The senior high youth fellowship responded by volunteering to wash coffee cups and silverware after coffee hour, since plastic foam cups and plastic forks were oil byproducts and added to the solid waste stream.

Adult members seemed pleased at first. Then the youth carried their environmental message one step further. They began placing informational posters next to the coffee cups and napkins. These posters routinely criticized the use of chemicals in farming and challenged other common practices in contemporary agriculture.

Unfortunately, North Ridge sat in the middle of a valley where most members made their living in agribusiness. The youth's posters offended many of the congregation's farmers. They felt that the youth were presenting a one-sided view. Washing coffee cups was one thing. Openly challenging how they managed their farms was quite another.

One Tuesday in late November, Howard walked into Mike's office and demanded that Mike "do something immediately" about the youth group's environmental advocacy. Mike responded that he could not control the youth group.

After all, they had their own advisors. More important, they had as much right to express their opinions as anyone else. Howard answered angrily that he was the senior pastor and that he expected Mike to do as he was told.

Upset and angry, Mike called the youth group advisors and described his encounter with Howard. Later, Howard accused Mike of "stirring up opposition" to his ministry by telling the advisors what Howard had said and done. The advisors were outraged that Howard would try to silence their sons and daughters just to placate the congregation's prominent farm families. They immediately confronted Howard, accusing him of acting like a tyrant.

The conflict between Mike and Howard quickly escalated into an ugly church fight. North Ridge's membership shattered into conflicting groups. Some supported Howard, arguing that he was the pastor and had a right to set his staff's agenda. Others supported Mike, feeling that Howard had violated a basic principle of collegiality and collaboration.

The staff-parish relations committee, most of whom were Howard's close friends, clearly supported him. The district superintendent tended to think in terms of hierarchy and control. Just as he expected pastors to return forms and follow instructions, he thought North Ridge's staff should follow Howard's orders. At its March meeting, the staff-parish relations committee voted to request that the bishop reappoint Mike to another congregation. The district superintendent informed Mike in an interview that he would have difficulty finding Mike another appointment. He said that Mike had gained a reputation for insubordination and lack of respect for authority.

Mike felt deeply hurt and disillusioned. How could something that initially seemed so promising have ended so badly?

TOUCHED BY FIRE

"You'd better hurry over to the church," Chantelle said. "It's on fire." Leon Henry felt the room spin around him as he hung up the phone. When he stepped out of his car, Leon was not sure how he had driven to the church. He felt numb and disoriented. The red, blue, and yellow lights of fire trucks and police cars were blinking in the early evening light. Leon, along with other church members, stood silently as flames consumed Mt. Bethel Church's walls, engulfed its roof, and left it a heap of smoldering timbers and shingles.

Leon's immediate concern was to help Mt. Bethel's members grieve their loss, deal with their anger, and look to the future. As Leon thought about the future, he felt overwhelmed. Leon had been certified as a lay speaker two years earlier. When his district superintendent asked him to preach regularly at Mt. Bethel, a small open-country church in a rural county near his hometown, Leon leapt at the opportunity. Now he wondered how he could possibly help the congregation. He knew about preaching and praying with people. But how would he ever have the time—let alone the skills—to rebuild Mt. Bethel's sanctuary?

He had served on his home church's administrative board when they built a new education wing. He knew that all the work had fallen on the pastor's shoulders. Everyone had expected the pastor to make the decisions, answer the questions, and be responsible for the whole project. How would he ever find time to manage all these responsibilities for Mt. Bethel when he had another full-time job?

Leon soon found out that his fears were unfounded. At a special administrative council meeting immediately after the fire, Mt. Bethel's lay leadership told Leon not to worry. They would take charge of rebuilding their church. Leon's responsibility, they reminded him, was to help them find meaning in their loss, maintain a sense of community while they were without a building, and stay aware of the larger world's needs at a time when they would be tempted to focus too much on their own needs.

Over the next year, an effective partnership developed between Leon and Mt. Bethel's leaders. Leon experienced himself as a servant to the group, providing them with tools and ideas to help them do their work. When the new church building was dedicated, Leon and Mt. Bethel's leaders celebrated not only the rebuilding of their sanctuary but a renewed sense of their shared ministry.

THREE WAYS OF LEADING WITH POWER

In the Introduction (pages 5–12) we used biblical examples to identify three ways of leading with power: *power-over*, *power-within*, and *power-with*. The stories above describe present-day experiences of the three ways men and women lead with power. Each way is unique. Each has positive and negative aspects. We cannot say that one way is right and the others are wrong. Each has strengths and weaknesses.

LEADING WITH POWER FROM WITHIN

Norma and Sylvia illustrate how some leaders lead with *power-within*. They draw upon power that is rooted in expertise or personal qualities. Both Norma and Sylvia claim expertise that comes from a specialized theological education. Sylvia, in addition, appeals to her expertise as a former public school teacher. Both women also have strong personalities. They are articulate, intelligent, hardworking, and likable. Norma has power that derives from her fifty-year presence in the community.

Norma and Sylvia illustrate how ambiguous *power-within* can be. Both Norma and Sylvia feel tremendously empowered. Claiming their own unique gifts and graces for ministry releases creativity, energy, and imagination in both women. Yet this same *power-within* also disempowers others. Norma's strong leadership of the UMW prevents other women from developing their own gifts as leaders. The group consequently struggles to survive after Norma resigns. Sylvia appeals to her expertise in Christian religious education in order to silence opposition to her proposed changes in confirmation. Faced with her appeal to special expertise and personal experience, the education committee passively accepts Sylvia's leadership.

LEADING WITH *POWER-OVER*

The conflict between Howard Parker and Mike Scott goes beyond two strong personalities who claim *power-within*. Their conflict draws our attention to a second type of power to lead: *power-over*. Howard, as Mike's senior pastor, has significant authority or positional power over Mike. Howard's power to lead is legitimated by recognized offices—the bishop and the district superintendent. Howard uses this positional power over Mike effectively, if destructively, in their escalating conflict. Howard also has access to other forms of power because he is Mike's superior in a clearly defined bureaucratic structure. He can mobilize the staff-parish relations committee, for example.

Power-over expresses itself through positional authority that derives from a leader's social location in a hierarchy or organizational structure. Howard clearly possesses this type of *power-over*. Howard's relationship with Mike also illustrates a second expression of *power-over*. Howard plays a parental role in relation to Mike. He is old enough to be Mike's father. Indeed, Mike perceives Howard as a parental figure in his life long before he arrives at North Ridge Church. Perhaps no relationship more clearly signifies *power-over* than this parental role. It is possible that this parent–child dynamic between Howard and Mike accounts for some of Howard's expectations of obedience and Mike's resistance to Howard's *power-over* authority.

Power-over, like *power-within*, has both positive and negative aspects. Howard's positional power initially provides Mike's ministry with a sense of legitimacy. It authorizes Mike for action. Howard uses his institutionally legitimated power to empower Mike's ministry. The destructive aspects of *power-over* surface later, as the conflict between Howard and Mike escalates. Howard eventually uses his power over North Ridge Church to control and to coerce. This tendency to manipulate, dominate, and control represents the dark side of *power-over*.

Mike, despite his rejection of Howard's way of leading, relies upon the same positional power over others to accomplish his work as associate pastor. By virtue of his office, Mike mobilizes resources and directs attention to certain issues.

The same dynamics apply to parental expressions of *power-over*. As a parent, I can use my generational authority to protect my children from danger, to infuse values into their lives, or to guide them toward autonomy. Howard, at the beginning of Mike's ministry, seems to play this role. On the other hand, a parent can use his or her generational authority to control, manipulate, and dominate. As events unfold at North Ridge Church, Howard's power over Mike takes this darker, more ominous turn.

Both *power-over* and *power-within* are ambiguous ways to lead. Held firmly within a particular range of expression, they have positive effects. Carried beyond this zone of effectiveness, they become destructive and disempower others.

LEADING WITH THE POWER OF COLLABORATION

Leon Henry's story draws our attention to a third way to lead with power. Leon's power to lead does not derive from his personal qualities or from his expertise. It does not stem from an official position Leon holds, although he is a certified lay speaker. Both Leon and Mt. Bethel's leaders exercise mutual or co-active power. Leon exercises this *power-with* by serving Mt. Bethel's leadership team. He gives this team the tools and resources its members need to accomplish the tasks that they define as important. Leon's role is to be a servant and a partner. In Leon's case, leading with power does not mean emphasizing his own expertise or personal charisma. Nor does it involve appeals to the authority of his office or church position. Instead, leading with power entails mutuality, reciprocity, and shared responsibility.

As with our other two ways of leading with power, this approach has both possibilities and dangers. *Power-with* can be tremendously empowering. At Mt. Bethel it releases unanticipated energy. Yet Mt. Bethel's story also provides an insight into the dangers of leading with collaborative power. Mt. Bethel's leaders worry that the effort to rebuild their house of worship will turn the congregation inward upon itself.

Precisely because leading with the power of collaboration places a high priority on relationships and friendships, it runs the risk of becoming exclusive and self-limiting. The emphasis falls upon fellowship rather than service. The enjoyment of friendship among like-minded people supersedes mission, witness, and service to the larger world.

THE PROMISE AND PERIL OF LEADING WITH POWER

We have thus identified at least three ways to lead with power. Some leaders rely on their personal charisma or their expertise, exercising *power-within*. This form of power can be empowering to the person exercising it. It releases creativity and energy. It challenges traditional ways of doing things.

Yet *power-within* can also disempower others. Charismatic leaders have such a strong need to employ their gifts that others lack the space to develop their own gifts. The charismatic leader's need to demonstrate expertise is so strong that other voices are silenced and disempowered. Such leaders easily fall into the trap of becoming celebrities rather than servants.

Others prefer to lead with *power-over*. They rely on positional power or the authority of their office. Like *power-within*, *power-over* can be used to empower others. On the other hand, leaders can use *power-over* in ways that manipulate and coerce.

Finally, *power-with* finds expression in leaders who value collaboration and mutuality. This way of leading with power can also be immensely generative. As people work collaboratively, new ideas surface that no single individual could have imagined. Synergy develops, and the Spirit carries people where they never dreamed possible.

On the other hand, *power-with* can turn groups inward. They can become so invested in their own interactions that they fail to see the larger world around them. They lose the capacity for servanthood, which is a catalyst for partnerships in the gospel.

No easy answer exists for how to lead with power. No single way is the only right way to be a leader. Each has its unique assets and its distinctive liabilities. The key question is not which ways are right and which are wrong. The truly important issue is whether we are aware of our typical way of leading with power and its impact upon others. How do others expect us to lead with power? How do they lead with power? How do we prefer to lead with power? At what point do the particular strengths inherent in our unique way of leading drift into liabilities that undermine our basic intent as leaders?

QUESTIONS FOR REFLECTION

1. What experiences have you had that make you reluctant to be a leader in your congregation, district, conference, or community? What do those experiences tell you about your understanding of leadership?

2. What experiences have you had that inspire you to be a leader in your congregation, district, conference, or community? What do those experiences tell you about your understanding of leadership?

3. Describe some individuals who have led with power from within (personal qualities, expertise). How did you experience them as leaders? In what ways did their leadership empower you and others? In what ways did it disempower you and others?

4. Describe some individuals who have led with *power-over* (positional, parental). How did you experience them as leaders? In what ways did their leadership empower you and others? In what ways did it disempower you and others?

5. Describe some individuals who have led with power that is collaborative and mutual. How did you experience them as leaders? In what ways did their leadership empower you and others? In what ways did it disempower you and others?

6. As you think about your own way of leading with power, are you more likely to rely on personal power from within, on

positional or parental power over others, or on co-active power? What effects do you believe your leadership has on you? on others?

Chapter Two

Rethinking Leadership

Most of us think that leadership is what leaders do. "Our pastor is really providing leadership for the evangelism program," a church member says. "Betsy has real leadership potential," a member of the nominations and personnel committee remarks. These comments imply that leadership is something leaders *do*. They suggest that leadership is a personal quality belonging to individual leaders.

If you are an attentive reader, however, you may have noticed that I have not used the word *leadership* to describe what leaders do. Leaders may use power to accomplish goals and achieve purposes, but leading with power is different from exercising leadership. They are certainly related, but they are not the same thing.

Until about one hundred years ago, the English language did not commonly use the word *leadership*. People spoke about leading and leaders. They did not speak about leadership. The term *leadership* became popular only at the end of the nineteenth century, particularly in North America. Its popularity increased immensely during the twentieth century. We now talk endlessly about leadership but less frequently about leading. The noun has replaced the verb. The state or condition of leadership has superseded the activity of leading.[2]

LEADERSHIP AS A RELATIONSHIP

Leadership—contrary to our usual assumptions—is not a possession that leaders pass around like a baton or a hand grenade. It is not a piece of property that leaders own. It is not a state of being or a condition. It is instead an active relationship in which leaders participate.

Norma, Sylvia, Howard, Mike, and Leon all illustrate different ways in which individuals lead with power. Despite their differences, they have one thing in common: *Their power to lead derives from the relationships in which they participate.* None of these leaders operates in a vacuum. All of them lead with power—albeit different kinds of power—because they share in relationships of mutual influence with others. Leadership, above all else, is a relationship.

Norma Knight's power to lead emerges from within. It is based on personal charisma and expertise. But her *power-within* remains authoritative only so long as others recognize its potency and relevancy. Faith Church's members must validate her gifts and recognize her as their leader. Norma must continue to impress Faith Church's members with her spiritual gifts in order to maintain her role as their leader. More important, Faith Church's members must be willing to be impressed! Norma's role as leader ultimately depends upon her relationship with the people at Faith Church. Although Norma's power to lead comes from within, it remains effective only because both she and Faith Church's members participate in a leadership relationship. Each party contributes something and receives something. Without this relationship between them, leadership would not be possible.

The rift between Sylvia and Norma reflects leadership's relational basis. Norma's power to lead is gradually weakened as Faith Church's members enter into a deeper and more dynamic relationship with Sylvia. As Sylvia builds relationships based on mutual influence and common purposes with Faith Church's members, a flow of leadership develops. This flow of leadership challenges and perhaps threatens Norma's own leadership relationship with the people of Faith Church.

At first glance, Howard Parker appears to have accumulated various packets or bundles of power: his role as senior pastor, his status in the district and conference, his positional authority over Mike. He then uses these power packets to lead. Howard triumphs over Mike, we might conclude, because he possesses more of these power packets.

Yet even Howard's ability to lead with *power-over* ultimately relies upon a network of relationships. Howard's power to lead depends upon his relationship with prominent members at North Ridge Church. Even Howard recognizes the importance of these relationships. When the youth fellowship's eco-justice campaign offends powerful families, Howard responds immediately. He recognizes that his ability to lead with *power-over* hinges upon his relationships with North Ridge's powerful farm families. Power is never the property of an individual, not even someone as authoritative as Howard. It ultimately belongs to a group. To say that Howard is "in power" is to say that North Ridge's leading families have empowered him to act on their behalf.

The most obvious example of leadership's relational basis is Leon Henry's exercise of *power-with*. *Power-with* reveals the relational foundation upon which all leadership ultimately rests. Its emphasis upon collaboration and mutuality makes this way of leading with power transparent to its relational foundations.

But we must not conclude that of the three ways to lead with power, *power-with* is the only way that possesses a relational basis. As we have already noted, all three ways of leading with power depend upon relationships to one degree or another. This relational basis is simply more obvious when people lead with *power-with*.

LEADERSHIP IS NOT A PERSONAL QUALITY

Leadership, then, is not a personal quality possessed by individuals; yet we continue to speak of leadership in precisely this way. "Amanda has leadership ability," we say. Or we criticize a pastor, complaining that "he just lacks leadership." People often equate leadership with influence, authority, impact, or prominence. The problem with such definitions is that they carry hidden assumptions about how people see themselves and, more important, how people believe that organizations make progress in dealing with the challenges facing them.

We can personally avoid the hard work of changing ourselves and our institutions when we define leadership as something that a handful of powerful individual leaders do. By defining leadership as an individual leader's responsibility, we make one person—the leader—responsible for the whole community's work. The rest of us are then absolved from any responsibility for our community's challenges, opportunities, and problems. We are merely followers, spectators who watch from a distance as great men and women transform the world.

By treating leadership as a personal possession, we transform leaders into celebrities and then expect them to dazzle and entertain us. To say that leaders do leadership is to direct our attention away from ourselves and the shared challenges we face. We instead focus our gaze on what a few prominent, influential, or authoritative individuals do and say.

Such a perspective fosters both self-delusion and irresponsibility. It encourages grandiosity and celebrity-seeking in those appointed as our leaders. They begin to believe that they really are the only ones who make things happen. This perspective on leadership also entices us to abdicate our responsibility for the hard work of changing and serving our world. When we see critical problems facing our congregations, we shrug our shoulders and say, "What can I do? I'm not the leader." Committee members sit back and "watch the elephants trample the grass" as powerful church members struggle for dominance.

LEADERSHIP IS NOT A POWER PACKET

A very different perspective comes into view when we see leadership as a relationship of mutual influence in which partners intend to make real changes that reflect mutual purposes. Such a definition suggests that we are all responsible for helping change ourselves, our congregations, and our world.

Leaders do not "do leadership" while followers "do followership." Leadership is not a distant, magical force that a few leaders possess but the rest of us lack. It is a dynamic between people, all of whom have power. Leaders and followers are partners in this dynamic dance; together they "do leadership." Leaders and followers together form one relationship that is leadership—a leadership relationship.

Leadership is a way of interacting. It is not a possession—a power packet—but a process, not a state or condition but an interactive activity. To confuse leadership with a leader is to confuse a process with a person. When my sons and I walk through the woods near our home, we often find deer tracks in the soft earth. One of us will point and say, "Look, a deer must have been through here today." We never confuse the deer with their tracks. We never point to the tracks and say, "Oh, look, I see a deer." Yet this is precisely what we do when we confuse the *effects* of leadership with the *activity* of leadership itself. We see events and behaviors but overlook the patterns and processes that created these events. We see the use of power but fail to notice the more fundamental, systemic relationships out of which this exercise of power has emerged. Although leadership is a relational circle of mutual influence and empowerment, we see only the straight line of people, events, behaviors.

This relationship of influence that we call leadership is multidimensional. The leader influences followers. Followers, in turn, influence their leader. While influence may be mutual and multidimensional, it is not equal. The patterns of power give the leader greater influence than the followers.

Once we see leadership as a relationship of mutual influence, then sharp contrasts between leaders and followers disappear. Leaders cannot exist without followers; followers cease to exist without leaders. Leaders and followers exchange roles over time and in different settings. People serve simultaneously as both leaders and followers. Leadership thus depends ultimately upon mutuality, collaboration, egalitarian relationships, and open dialogue.

LEADERSHIP REQUIRES MUTUAL PURPOSES

The terms *leaders* and *followers*, in fact, do not truly capture this dynamic give-and-take relationship. We might better describe participants as *partners* than as leaders and followers. Partners can exchange roles. Partners each give and receive something from their relationships. Partners are bound together by mutual purposes and shared intentions.

Mutual purposes are forged through the give-and-take of influence relationships. Mutual purposes evolve as people collaborate, engage in dialogue, and generate new meanings. Mutual purposes can never emerge in an atmosphere of coercion and manipulation. They demand a free, open, and hospitable space where people can collaborate on the creation of shared meaning and the generating of shared values.

Leon Henry and Mt. Bethel's members participate together in a leadership relationship that intends real changes reflecting mutual purposes. In the wake of Mt. Bethel's fire, Leon Henry and the congregation's lay leadership lead with co-active or mutual power. The church fire serves as a catalyst, stimulating everyone to clarify Mt. Bethel's purpose for being. This shared purpose guides the exercise of leadership by Leon and Mt. Bethel's laity.

In the same way, Norma Knight and Sylvia Canivez intend real changes that reflect mutual purposes. Both, for example, seek to introduce more inclusive language into Faith Church's worship. Both, along with Faith Church's leading families, share a common purpose of strong and effective educational programs for youth.

Howard Parker and Mike Scott, on the other hand, demonstrate the difference between mutual purposes and independent purposes mutually held. Howard and Mike have independent purposes that appear to be mutual. Both want a strong congregation. Both want an active education program. They assume they are working toward the same goals, but they never spend time talking about what they ultimately hope to create. In reality, each of them means something very different by "strong congregation" and "active education program." What Howard means by a strong education program clearly differs from what Mike means. As a result, their purposes are not truly mutual;

they really hold independent purposes. Because they lack truly mutual purposes, their relationship degenerates as soon as their underlying differences are unmasked.

If leadership is a relationship between leaders and followers, it cannot be done without a mutuality of purpose. Common purposes are not independent goals mutually held. Nor are common purposes concerned with immediate goals. Mutual or common purposes involve end-values such as compassion, service, witness, freedom, and peace. Mutually-held independent goals do not build community. Only mutual purposes commonly held can create and maintain communities.

LEADERSHIP AS A CHRISTIAN SOCIAL PRACTICE

If leadership is a dynamic relationship between people, then leadership is primarily a *social* practice—it is not a private activity. Leadership as a social practice (as we have seen in the stories of Norma, Sylvia, Howard, and Leon) varies widely from person to person and from situation to situation. Yet it always addresses the same fundamental human need for the ordering of human community. Social practices are concrete acts that address fundamental human needs and conditions. If we think about leadership as a Christian social practice, several themes begin to unfold.[3]

SOCIAL PRACTICES HAVE BOTH EXTERNAL OUTCOMES AND INHERENT WORTH

First, social practices are done for practical purposes. They result in concrete outcomes that enhance human life and community. Yet they also have their own inherent value. They are good activities in which to participate even when the outcomes are ambiguous or invisible. We somehow sense we are changed and transformed through our participation in these practices even when concrete results are absent.

I once lived in a community where we staged a rally each fall to support racial and economic justice. On one level, these rallies did not have many concrete outcomes. Racism still exists. Economic injustice continues. Yet even when no concrete outcomes happened because we rallied and marched, everyone viewed this activity as worthwhile. Something happened to us simply by being with others who cared about this issue. Our fall rally is an example of how social practices have external, concrete goals as well as values internal to the practice itself.

Church leadership as a social practice has both concrete, practical outcomes and values inherent in the activity of leading itself. Ministries are organized. Programs are celebrated. Buildings are constructed. Mission trips are organized. All these are concrete outcomes that result from leadership as a relationship between partners in the gospel who intend real changes based on mutual purposes. Leaders help congregations order members' gifts in ways that allow people to flourish and that encourage witness and mission to flower. Without the practice of leadership, congregations drift and founder.

Yet the practice of leadership entails more than such concrete outcomes. Even when our leadership efforts show no visible results, we still view them as worthwhile endeavors in which to participate. People may not respond to the congregation's new initiatives, but we know that something worthwhile has happened among us. We are not the same people as we were before. We know each other more deeply. We have made new connections between our faith and daily life. We see the world a little differently. Our experience of leadership tells us that the internal fruit of leadership makes the effort worthwhile even when concrete results are lacking.

SOCIAL PRACTICES ARE DONE TOGETHER WITH OTHERS OVER TIME

Second, social practices are activities that Christians do together over time. When we enter into a Christian social practice such as leadership, we discover that we are participating in something larger than ourselves. This practice began long ago. As we engage in this practice, our lives are woven together with those of others who have engaged, are engaging, or will engage in this practice along with us. It is not something we invent and do alone. We do it in conversation with others.

We grow as leaders by reflecting with others on our practice of leadership. Some of our conversation partners are people distant from us in time and space. Others speak to us from our religious tradition: Moses, Miriam, Jacob, Deborah, Paul, Peter, Timothy, Joanna. Still others are people we know in our own congregation, district, conference, or community. We grow as leaders not only through having leadership experiences but also through thinking together with others about what we have done, are doing, and hope to do as leaders.

SOCIAL PRACTICES HAVE STANDARDS OF EXCELLENCE

Third, social practices possess standards of excellence. Some ways of leading result in more faithful ways of being in community than do others. Norma Knight, Sylvia Canivez, Howard Parker, Mike Scott, and Leon Henry all engage in the practice of leadership with varying levels of excellence. How we evaluate their performance may, in part, depend upon our own values and perspectives. What we say about them may reveal more about us than it tells about them.

All of us have unspoken assumptions about what constitutes good leadership. Howard Parker, for example, perceived no discrepancy between what he preached from the pulpit about shared ministry and how he used his positional power over Mike. We need to ask ourselves constantly how well we are fulfilling our own standards of excellence in leadership. Faithful leadership also requires that we ask ourselves what we unconsciously assume constitutes good leadership.

FAITHFUL LEADERSHIP AS SERVANTHOOD

What standards of excellence do we apply when we judge leadership's faithfulness as a Christian social practice? How do we know when we are leading faithfully *as Christians*? One possible standard of excellence is servanthood.

Like leadership, servanthood is a relational concept. Service requires two or more people. Some are serving. Others are served. Like leadership, service is a social practice. It is something that has both practical outcomes and inherent value for its own sake. Like leadership, servanthood has its own standards of excellence. We all know what excellent service looks and feels like.

Servanthood and leadership, then, are interrelated practices. We can better appreciate what faithful Christian leadership looks like by understanding servanthood. Conversely, we more fully grasp the nature of service as we examine it through the lens of leadership. Those who lead with power participate in true and faithful leadership when they see themselves as leaders who are also servants.

Leadership thrives only when all participants are willing to be servants to one another and to the process of leadership itself. We witness faithful leadership when everyone practices mutual service toward one another. Excellence in leadership also requires that all involved see themselves as servants not only to one another but also to the mutual purposes that bind them together.

At one point in my life, I believed that the only legitimate way to lead with power was through the exercise of *power-with*. Neither *power-over* nor *power-within*, I concluded, was a legitimate way to exercise leadership. Gradually my views have changed. I have come to see that the exercise of *power-over* or *power-within* is not always illegitimate and abusive. Similarly, I have discovered that even *power-with* can be exercised in ways that diminish life and stunt growth.

Servanthood purifies the exercise of *power-over*. *Power-over* expresses its dark side as dominance and control. We expect to be served, not to serve. The relationship only moves in one direction. Others serve us; we dominate them. When this happens, we may lead with power, but leadership is absent from the congregation. Leadership is relational. It requires mutual service. Servanthood reminds leaders that inequality is a temporary condition—the ultimate goal is *mutual* service.

Servanthood also cleanses *power-within* of its tendency to demand center stage and to marginalize other people and disempower them of their gifts. It reminds leaders, no matter what their personal charisma or expertise, that they do not possess all the gifts needed for a congregation's total witness. Even experts and those with powerful personalities sometimes need to be served as well as to serve. Emphasizing our own autonomy prevents mutuality in serving and being served. When we mutually serve each other, I can influence you as well as be influenced by you. I feel equally powerful whether I am influencing or am being influenced. I recognize that true power ultimately resides neither in you nor in me—it exists in our mutual interaction with each other. The power we share increases my own sense of strength as well as yours. Servanthood transforms my leading with *power-within* into a leadership relationship in which I participate along with you in making real changes that reflect mutually held purposes.

Finally, servanthood redeems *power-with* of the temptation to become exclusive, inwardly focused, and elitist. It challenges those in leadership relationships to remember that God has not gifted their religious community so that people can enjoy one another's company. God has gifted the community with power so that those for whom Christ came as a servant may still be served.

SERVANTHOOD AND THE PURIFICATION OF *POWER-OVER*

Becoming a parent forced me to reconsider my negative evaluation of *power-over*. As a parent, I experience situations in which I legitimately need to lead with power over my children. A few years ago, our family went on a vacation to Arizona. I was shocked, as the parent of two toddlers, to realize that there were only minimal guardrails at some of the overlooks to the Grand Canyon! As my three-year-old son ran toward the rail, I exercised *power-over*, firmly telling him to hold my hand and stay near me. In that moment I realized that *power-over* could be exercised in ways that sustain life, not just distort it.

Parenting, after all, is a form of leadership. It can be—and in certain cases certainly is—abusive and manipulative. Yet at its best it illustrates what the positive face of *power-over* can be. It protects life, sets boundaries, and fosters growth. It ultimately encourages independence and freedom. Good parents do not want to keep their children in permanent dependency. Their ultimate goal is a relationship between equals. The inequality is always treated as a temporary condition that will give way to true mutuality and equality as children mature into adulthood.

I also exercise *power-over* when I teach. Teaching, like parenting, can degenerate into an opportunity to dominate, intimidate, and overwhelm. Yet at its best, teaching can include teachers who lead with *power-over* in the service of the learner's growth and freedom. Again, the key to the relationship is understanding that any inequality between teachers and students is a temporary condition. Good teachers, like good mentors, always envision a time when their students will be equal partners with them.

A leader's exercise of *power-over* is not necessarily coercive, manipulative, or abusive. Unfortunately, most of our experiences with *power-over* have been negative ones. So we avoid leading with *power-over*. It is so tainted with coercion that we do not want to be involved with it. We overlook the possibility that *power-over* can be wielded in ways that foster growth and that help us order activities in ways that promote freedom.

Many leaders who exercise *power-over* frequently promise precisely such care but then deliver only control. I may claim I am serving my three-year-old son by protecting his life, yet my real interest may be to dominate and control him. I claim that as a teacher I am fostering learners' growth, yet what I am really doing is overwhelming and intimidating them. Leading with *power-over* can become paternalistic. It promises care but delivers dependency. We are protected at the expense of our own growth.

This potential for abuse always exists when we lead with *power-over*. Yet *power-over* can sometimes be a legitimate expression of leadership. What makes the difference? How do we determine whether a particular expression of *power-over* has been faithful? What standards of excellence help us judge *power-over*?

Servanthood becomes the standard of excellence by which we may judge the performance of those who lead with *power-*

over. Leading with *power-over* is faithful when the leader is motivated by servanthood. When I see myself as a servant temporarily exercising *power-over* in order to cultivate a context where eventually we can be equals and mutual partners, then my power to lead does not degenerate into manipulation and coercion.

Servanthood reminds leaders that the inequality in a *power-over* relationship is only temporary, not terminal. Servanthood is full of surprising reversals and transformations. Right now we may be the ones serving. Tomorrow, we will be served. When we keep in mind that our power over others is only temporary, we are more likely to use it with care, consideration, and justice. Servanthood transforms our leading with *power-over* into faithful leadership that is purified of its tendency to dominate and control.

Howard, for example, appears not to have envisioned a time when he and Mike would be in a relationship of equals. Howard was old enough to be Mike's father. He was ending his career. Mike was only beginning his ministry. Howard did not see Mike as someone whom he could mentor and guide into ministry. He inquired about Mike's ministry at the Monday staff meetings. Beyond these brief inquiries, however, he showed little interest in Mike. In this sense, Howard's exercise of power over Mike—a power that was certainly his as senior pastor—was not tempered by servanthood. He did not see himself as serving Mike as a mentor and guide. Nor did he envision a time when Mike would be his equal partner in a relationship of serving and being served.

Servanthood tempers the exercise of *power-over* in a second way. Whatever external inequality of power may seem to exist between people, *power-over* is legitimate when both leaders and followers see themselves in mutual service to the common purposes that unite them. Both partners in the leadership relationship are committed to the same purposes. Leaders are not interested in having people serve their needs. Instead, leaders seek to serve, along with others, the common purposes that unite them. The exercise of *power-over* is set within this framework of service to a larger, commonly shared purpose.

Howard and Mike lack this sense of mutual service to a common purpose. Howard shows little interest in what Mike is doing or hopes to do with North Ridge's education program. Mike, for his part, never asks Howard how he sees education as fitting into some larger vision of North Ridge Church's mission. They exercise their ministries independently of each other. Without this sense of being in mutual service to a commonly held larger purpose, Howard's exercise of power over Mike can easily drift into coercion and domination. Howard has the power to lead, but North Ridge Church still lacks faithful leadership, a relationship of mutual influence between partners in the gospel who intend real changes that reflect common purposes.

It is both unrealistic and dangerous to expect people invested with *power-over* by virtue of their official position to refuse to use this positional power. Congregations expect leaders to lead. Denigrating the validity of *power-over* only weakens congregations, many of which already experience an absence of leaders and leadership. A better path is to encourage those vested with *power-over* through their election to church boards and committees, to lead with power—but to do so as servants. Seeing themselves as servants helps leaders purify their exercise of *power-over* of its destructive potential.

SERVANTHOOD AND THE CLEANSING OF *POWER-WITHIN*

Servanthood also helps us distinguish between *power-within* that is destructive and *power-within* that is life-giving. When leaders exercise *power-within* without a sense of being servants, they can easily drift into believing that they personally possess everything necessary for effective and faithful ministry. They need nothing from others. They consequently leave no room for other church members to discover and use their own unique gifts for ministry.

Norma Knight demonstrates this exercise of *power-within* that lacks any sense of servanthood. Norma's considerable gifts so dominate Faith Church's UMW that no one else's gifts have an opportunity to blossom. The UMW nearly disbands without Norma's presence. Norma appears to lead in ways that encourage others to look upon her with admiration and deference. She enjoys being the center of the Easter sunrise service. She enjoys the attention that Faith Church's members give to her. She uses her considerable gifts not to serve others but to prop up her own position and self-image. She does not use her gifts to educate, energize, and empower others. Norma's domination is so complete that she allows no other leaders to emerge.

Leaders who possess considerable *power-within* are sometimes tempted to believe that they are the only people with gifts and graces for ministry. These leaders want to serve but not be served. People who exercise *power-within* need to be reminded that they are not the only ones with gifts. They are not above being served by others. Rather, they exercise their gifts in a community of equals where all are servants to one another.

Servanthood involves humility. Humility serves as a check on *power-within*'s tendency to focus on the leader's autonomy and self-sufficiency. It dispels the illusion that everything depends on the charismatic leader or the expert. Servanthood reminds leaders that their gifts have not been given so that they can be the object of everyone's admiration and praise. Rather, God has bestowed these gifts for the sake of service to others.

Again, we are being irresponsible if we discount the importance of individuals with special expertise or unique spiritual gifts. If we suggest that those who lead with *power-within* are not faithful leaders, we are depriving the church of important gifts for ministry. We are also devaluing the skills and talents of gifted individuals. A better solution is to appreciate those who lead with *power-within* and to urge them to set their gifts within a framework of servanthood.

SERVANTHOOD AND THE REDEMPTION OF *POWER-WITH*

Power-with can sometimes degenerate into exclusiveness and elitism. Groups can become bogged down in process and relationship. Nothing actually happens because people are too busy relating to one another. Intimacy for its own sake becomes the goal. The leader becomes a terminal facilitator, just another member of the group enjoying the relationships and enabling a process that seems to have no purpose and no end. Leadership characterized by the exercise of *power-with* can reduce the leader's function, denying that he or she has any special role to play or task to fulfill.

This danger existed at Mt. Bethel. Mt. Bethel was a small rural congregation. Members were content to enjoy their relationships with one another. Leon Henry was a part-time pastor who, as a lay speaker, could easily slip into the role of just another member of the community.

Servanthood serves as a brake upon these tendencies inherent in *power-with*. Servanthood reminds leaders that they have a particular role and task in their communities, that they are not just another member of the group. Leaders have a responsibility to serve their congregations. They have the unique responsibility of helping members collectively acknowledge the challenges facing them, reflect on their present values and behaviors, make decisions in light of these reflections, and take joint action. Leaders are a special category of servants. They are more akin to stewards. They manage the household in the master's absence, making all necessary arrangements so that the household as a whole is well-ordered.

Furthermore, servanthood reminds communities characterized by *power-with* that they do not exist simply to enjoy one another's company. Congregations exist within larger communities where the hungry need to be fed, the naked clothed, and the marginalized made welcome. God calls congregations to make disciples, to proclaim the good news, to bear witness to the faith. Servanthood draws congregations out of their comfortable cocoons. It challenges them to serve the people for whom Christ the Servant lived, died, and was raised to new life.

SERVANTHOOD AS THE STANDARD FOR CHRISTIAN LEADERSHIP

If leadership as a Christian social practice has standards of excellence, these standards rest upon a foundation of servanthood. Regardless of how leaders exercise their power—as *power-over*, *power-with*, or *power-within*—the absence or presence of servanthood determines the ultimate effects upon both leader and constituents. (See Figure 1, page 51.)

Many of us seek a how-to recipe for leadership. We want to know what our "leadership style" is. We want some quick steps for being faithful leaders in every situation. However, many different ways of leading are possible. Faithful leadership does not depend on how we individually lead with power. It depends upon whether we are leading as servants. Servanthood transforms leading with power into leadership as a relationship of mutual influence between partners in the gospel who intend real changes that reflect common purposes.

QUESTIONS FOR REFLECTION

1. This chapter defines leadership as a relationship between leaders and constituents that involves mutual influence and intends real changes that reflect common purposes. How do you think about leadership? Have you thought of leadership as a personal quality of individuals? Does defining leadership as a relationship suggest new possibilities or shed new light on your experience?

2. What are some of the things that are inherently good about participating in leadership, regardless of whether the concrete outcomes are what we expect? How does being a leader change you?

3. Give some examples from your own experience of how the presence or absence of servanthood made a difference in leaders who exercised *power-over*?

4. Give some examples from your own experience of how the presence or absence of servanthood made a difference in leaders who exercised *power-within*?

5. Give some examples from your own experience of how the presence or absence of servanthood made a difference in leaders who exercised *power-with*?

6. This chapter identifies three ways servanthood influences leading with power. Can you think of additional ways?

Figure 1

Type of Power	Definition	Without Servant-hood	With Servant-hood
Power-over	Positional power; Bureaucratic office	Coercive; Manipulative; Uses power to achieve own ends; Not willing to serve others	Sees inequality as temporary; Uses power to achieve shared purposes; Willing to serve and be served
Power-within	Expertise; Charisma	Wants to serve, not be served; Uses power to make self the center of attention; Disempowers	Willing to be served as well as to serve; Uses power to strengthen others; Empowers others
Power-with	Mutuality; Relationship	Erases difference between leader and group; Exclusivism; Elitism	Leader as steward; Turns outward in service to outsiders

Chapter Three

I Give You a New Commandment

Above my grandfather's roll-top desk hung a copy of da Vinci's *The Last Supper*. In the painting, Jesus sits at the center of a long table spread with bread and wine. His disciples are gathered around him. Jesus is surrounded by those whom he loves, has forgiven, and has opened for communion with himself and one another.

The painting is full of the vitality and energy that radiate outward from those gathered as friends around Jesus' table. Jesus' power to lead, da Vinci hints, emerges from mutuality and meeting, from friendship and partnership. Leadership happens whenever we gather in mutuality and equality around the table of God. The power of the gospel, da Vinci implies, is *power-with*.

Whenever my family gathered for dinners, I saw that painting. As I reflect back, I realize how much it influenced my understanding of Jesus. More importantly, it shaped my own self-understanding as a church leader. In my mind's eye, I see Jesus surrounded by his friends. Jesus' table fellowship models how I am to lead. Like Jesus, I lead through mutuality and collaboration.

Another childhood image of Jesus also echoes in my memory. I grew up in a large old farmhouse in the country. My bedroom was on the second floor, far from the rest of the house. Like many children, I was afraid of the dark. To reassure me when I awoke in the middle of the night, my parents hung a small ceramic tile near my bed. I could see it from my pillow. When the light was on, I watched Jesus walking on the waves, stilling the storm. Once the lights were out, the fluorescent glow of a Latin cross mysteriously shone from the tile. When I awakened in the middle of the night, I saw the cross glowing in the darkness. It reassured me that I was not alone. The One who stilled the storm and quieted the waves was with me. He quieted my fears and stilled my racing thoughts. Jesus possessed a *power-within* that calmed the sea, healed the sick, and raised the dead to life.

To this day my image of Jesus is linked to this childhood memory. I experience Jesus as a spirit-person. He is a conduit of God's power and presence. He is a charismatic leader through whom God's spiritual power manifests itself. His contemporaries recognized him as a powerful leader because he possessed these charismatic gifts. They acknowledged him as having authority because he led with *power-within*.

I continue to judge faithful leadership by this same quality of *power-within*. I believe that faithful leaders are people whose spiritual lives enable them to tap into the power of God. Very early in my ministry I sought out a spiritual director and struggled to shape an appropriate spiritual discipline for myself.

Yet these are not the only images of Jesus that I have encountered in my spiritual journey. Some years ago I traveled the eastern Mediterranean. Visiting Greek Orthodox churches, I would look up and see, staring down at me from the ceiling, Jesus the Pantocrator, a word meaning almighty or all-governing. Jesus is no longer a friend seated among his companions. Nor is he a charismatic healer and teacher. He is a monarch clothed in royal robes, looking down upon me and all creation. He is the very embodiment of *power-over*.

A friend who studies Christian art once told me that many of the motifs in Greek Orthodox iconography are drawn from the royal rituals of the Byzantine court. Some icons, for example, show the women covering their hands with their garments as they approach Jesus. Why this curious detail? The answer lies in the fusion of Jesus with the emperor. When women came before the Byzantine emperor, they covered their hands with their robes as a sign of deference and submission. The emperor's absolute power to rule and control is interwoven with the image of Jesus the Pantocrator, who dominates all creation. Unfortunately, this same image of Jesus the King has authorized powerful church leaders to assume they could operate like little emperors with the power to control and dominate, manipulate and coerce.

HOW WE LEAD IS HOW WE SEE JESUS

How we envision Jesus as a leader shapes our own self-understanding as leaders. If we see Jesus as a friend to sinners, calling together a community where divine power mysteriously moves among a people of God, then we emphasize *power-with*. We, in turn, lead with the co-active power of mutuality and collaboration. If we see Jesus as a charismatic figure possessing special powers and gifts, we then believe that faithful leadership takes the form of *power-within*, involving personal charisma or expertise. Still others of us picture Jesus as a powerful ruler. So we take this image of *power-over* as our model for how faithful leaders act.

We find it hard to alter our practice of leadership precisely because our notions about leadership are closely related to our conceptions of Jesus. To change how we lead is not just a matter of changing a few behaviors and learning some new skills. Changing how we lead involves changing our picture of Jesus. Leadership is less about behaviors and techniques than about values and beliefs.

The relationship between our image of Jesus and our notion of leadership accounts for why we have such strong feelings about what constitutes good or bad leadership. Our experiences of leadership go to the heart of how we experience God in Christ. People who lead differently than we do are not just challenging our practice of leadership; they are also calling into question our understanding of Jesus.

FOCUSING ON ONLY ONE MODEL OF JESUS RESULTS IN UNIDIMENSIONAL LEADERSHIP

Art, music, and literature have at various points in church history overemphasized one or another of the three ways of leading with power. We too are tempted to move our three ways of leading with power beyond their zone of effectiveness. They cease being practices that generate leadership and instead become destructive and harmful.

One group of Christians sees Jesus only as the King who rules from his heavenly throne, controlling and directing all things with mighty *power-over*. They are also unconsciously authorizing their earthly leaders to rule with this same dominating *power-over*. Church leaders rule as little emperors whose every word is to be obeyed. Leaders seek maximum influence over others with minimum influence upon themselves. They lead competitively and adversarially with the aim of mastery or control.

Other Christians picture Jesus as a charismatic leader who possesses *power-within*. They consequently authorize church leaders with special gifts or expertise to monopolize their congregations. They allow a few strong leaders to be the focus of everyone's attention. Meanwhile, other members' gifts and talents are overlooked and underutilized.

Finally, still other Christians paint a portrait of Jesus as friend and companion who exercises *power-with*. They then apply this standard to their own church leaders. They inadvertently reduce their appointed leaders to terminal facilitators. They turn inward, focusing too much on their relationships with one another.

Our error lies in overlooking the rich diversity of how Jesus leads. We cannot reduce Jesus to one way of leading with power. The key to faithful leadership does not lie in focusing overly on one way of leading with power. It resides in understanding how service and servanthood transform all expressions of leading with power into genuine leadership.

Rather than elevate one way of leading with power as the *only* Christian way to lead, we need to see all three ways as existing in tension with one another. Faithful leaders can lead with any form of power, just as Jesus' own ministry demonstrates all three ways of leading with power. The fundamental issue is not which way of leading with power is right and which is wrong. The key question is whether our particular way of leading with power is appropriate to the situation and infused with the same spirit of service and servanthood that characterized Jesus' ministry.

SERVANTHOOD AS CENTRAL TO HOW JESUS LEADS WITH POWER

My six-year-old son, Robert, and I were driving home together after Maundy Thursday worship. Robert was thinking about the hymns we had sung and the Scriptures we had read. He was trying to understand the meaning of what he had experienced as the congregation washed feet and celebrated the Lord's Supper. "Jesus is a king," he said to me thoughtfully. "But I think Jesus' throne is the cross," he concluded.

Jesus' cross is his throne. Jesus is the Christ, the royal Messiah,

> who, though he was in the form of God,
>   did not regard equality with God
>   as something to be exploited,
> but emptied himself,
>   taking the form of a slave,
>   being born in human likeness.
> And being found in human form,
>   he humbled himself
>   and became obedient to the point of death—
>   even death on a cross. (Philippians 2:6-8)

The cross is Jesus' final act of service in a whole ministry characterized by servanthood.

Jesus leads with power. His power to lead finds its ultimate expression not in a throne but in a cross. Jesus' lordship comes to fruition not through domination and coercion but through humility and service.

JESUS' SERVANTHOOD AND *POWER-OVER*

John's Gospel records that Jesus got up from the table, took off his outer garment, tied a towel around his waist, and washed his disciples' feet. Provision for the washing of feet was typical hospitality in New Testament Palestine. Roads were dusty and dirty. People wore open sandals. Footwashing provided relief for hot and dusty feet.

Social status and power strongly influenced first-century Jewish social practices such as footwashing. To wash another person's feet was regarded as a menial task beneath all but the lowest social classes. According to Jewish customs of the time, a master could not even demand that his Jewish slave wash his feet. Guests were provided water but expected to wash their own feet.

Occasionally, as an act of love or devotion, someone might wash another's feet. In the tale of *Joseph and Aseneth*, an Alexandrian Jewish romance novel written between 100 B.C.E. (Before the Common Era) and 200 C.E. (Common Era), Aseneth bends down to wash Joseph's feet. When Joseph resists, not wanting to humiliate her, Aseneth tells him—in words that remind the reader of Ruth and Naomi—that his feet are her feet.

Similarly, Jewish disciples would occasionally wash their master's feet as a sign of devotion and humility. Rabbis were customarily served by their students. The underlying principle was that students learned the Torah (the Jewish Law) not just by listening to a teacher but through daily contact with him. This concrete daily interaction usually took the form of the students waiting on their master as his personal servants. Knowledge of the Torah could only be gained through service to the teacher. One rabbi supposedly went so far as to say that masters who prevented their students from serving them were denying them access to the Torah.

Jesus, however, reverses the meaning of footwashing. Although his disciples call him Teacher and Lord, he bends down and washes their feet. He then tells his disciples that they are to do as he has done. They are to become servants. "You call me Teacher and Lord—and you are right, for that is what I am. So if I, your Lord and Teacher, have washed your feet, you also ought to wash one another's feet" (John 13:13-14). This is Jesus' new commandment. This is the mandate from which

Maundy (meaning mandate) Thursday takes its name. "I give you a new commandment, that you love one another. Just as I have loved you, you also should love one another" (John 13:34).

Jesus clearly exercises power over his disciples. He is Lord and Teacher; they are novices, disciples who have come to learn from him. Yet Jesus' exercise of *power-over* does not degenerate into coercive domination. Servanthood excludes these abuses of *power-over*.

In Jesus' farewell discourse to his disciples, after he has washed their feet, he tells them:

> This is my commandment, that you love one another as I have loved you. . . . You are my friends if you do what I command you. I do not call you servants any longer, because the servant does not know what the master is doing; but I have called you friends, because I have made known to you everything that I have heard from my Father. . . . When the Advocate comes, whom I will send to you from the Father, the Spirit of truth who comes from the Father, he will testify on my behalf. You also are to testify because you have been with me from the beginning.
>
> (John 15:12, 14–15, 26–27)

These words from Jesus' farewell discourse recall two themes important to servanthood and *power-over* mentioned in Chapter Two.

First, although Jesus possesses power over his disciples as their Lord and Teacher, he looks beyond their temporary status of inequality. He envisions a relationship of mutual service among equals. This commitment to mutual service among equals, regardless of any present imbalance in power and influence, helps keep *power-over* from lapsing into control and domination. The goal is not mastery but meeting. *Power-over* is measured in terms of service rendered, not service acquired.

Second, Jesus exercises *power-over* within the framework of larger, shared purposes. Both he and his disciples share a common vision of making known God's glory. They are united through their mutual participation in God's larger purposes in human history. *Power-over* does not exist so that church leaders can use positional power to further their own personal agendas. It is used faithfully when church leaders employ it in service to larger, commonly shared purposes.

The criterion for faithful leadership becomes mutual and reciprocal enhancement of the community. Servant leaders administer church life in ways that benefit all the people, not just themselves. *Power-over* is tempered when all parties, including the leader, see themselves as servants to a larger purpose, a common vision, or a shared goal. A congregation once gave their departing pastor a plaque that said, "You made us do what we did not want to do so that we could become who we always wanted to be." This pastor used his positional power not to advance his personal goals but to accomplish mutually held purposes important to the congregation.

It is unreasonable to expect leaders placed in positions of authority to forego the legitimate exercise of *power-over*. *Power-over* is a necessary aspect of leading. We do a disservice to leaders when we demonize them for possessing *power-over*. To lay unnecessary guilt upon leaders who find themselves in positions of power over others is destructive and demoralizing. It distorts the exercise of leadership as a Christian social practice.

Church leaders are invested with *power-over* because churches, like all social organizations, require specialized offices to set direction, maintain boundaries, establish norms, and control conflict. The question is not whether leaders should possess *power-over.* The true challenge is to exercise this power within a leadership relationship between partners in the gospel who intend real changes reflecting common purposes.

When Good Shepherd's church conference elected Marge Cooper chair of a specially created long-range planning committee, Marge knew that she faced an overwhelming task. The committee's main responsibility was to examine the congregation's aging building and isolated location, determining whether the church would be best served by relocation to a new site or by remodeling of the current building.

Marge herself was a powerful leader. Members joked that she had held every office in the church except that of the preacher. She also owned a successful local business and had served on the city council. Despite her many resources for *power-over*, Marge was careful not to dominate the long-range planning committee. She appointed strong leaders to the sub-committees responsible for gathering information about various options. She encouraged members to speak frankly and openly. She never silenced viewpoints that opposed her own. She treated other committee members—even those who had only recently joined Good Shepherd Church—as her equals. Marge never used her power to set the agenda in order to manipulate information or influence decision-making.

Nor did Marge exploit her position to increase her own power and prestige in the congregation. She went quietly about her work. When others drew attention to her role in defining Good Shepherd's future, she redirected the conversation to shared values, hopes, and fears about the congregation's future. She kept the focus on Good Shepherd's future, not on what she was doing as committee chairperson.

Marge Cooper understood that *power-over* is an essential dimension of church life. Congregations require specially designated leaders who can guide decision-making and problem-solving processes. Yet, by exercising her *power-over* as a servant, Marge purged this power of its potential negativity. She thus ensured that it contributed to Good Shepherd's continuing faithfulness as a congregation.

This is surely what Jesus has in mind when he tells James and John that they are not to seek to be like the rulers of the Gentiles:

> You know that among the Gentiles those whom they recognize as their rulers lord it over them, and their great ones are tyrants over them. But it is not so among you; but whoever wishes to become great among you must be your servant, and whoever wishes to be first among you must be slave of all.
>
> (Mark 10:42-44)

Jesus does not tell James and John to avoid the responsibilities of leading others. He tells them they are to exercise their positional power and authority in ways unlike those in which rulers usually lead. When they lead with *power-over*, they do so as servants and not as tyrants.

JESUS' SERVANTHOOD AND *POWER-WITHIN*

Jesus was, without a doubt, a charismatic leader who possessed *power-within*. He went throughout Galilee, teaching and healing. Soon "his fame spread throughout all Syria" and "great crowds followed him from Galilee, the Decapolis, Jerusalem, Judea, and from beyond the Jordan" (Matthew 4:24, 25). Mark records how crowds were amazed at Jesus' teaching, "for he taught them as one having authority, and not as the scribes" (Mark 1:22). Mark uses the Greek word *exousia* to describe *power-within. Power-within* comes from out of (*ex*) one's being (*ousia*). Jesus has *power-within*, power that comes from out of his being.

The Gospels repeatedly describe Jesus as possessing special powers, particularly as a healer. When a woman secretly reaches out and touches Jesus as he passes by, he is "immediately aware that power had gone forth from him" (Mark 5:30). Jesus also has special expertise as a teacher of the Torah. He argues details of interpretation with the scribes and Pharisees. He points out inconsistencies in his opponents' arguments. He knows how to draw upon the resources of Scripture to drive home a point. Luke recounts how, even as a child, Jesus spent time in the Temple with the teachers of the Law (Luke 2:41-52).

This *power-within*, however, is exercised by one who sees himself first and foremost as a servant. Three qualities of servanthood shape Jesus' exercise of *power-within*. Two have already been mentioned in our discussion of *power-over*: First, servanthood envisions a time when all parties meet as equals engaged in mutual service. The leader treats any imbalance of power between leaders and others as a temporary condition. The ultimate goal is equality and mutual service. Second, servanthood encourages leaders to see themselves as engaged with others in the pursuit of larger, common purposes. We now add a third quality.

HUMILITY AND THE LEADER'S TEMPTATION TO BEDAZZLE

Humility constitutes the third quality of servanthood. It is particularly relevant to the exercise of *power-within*. As we mentioned in Chapter Two, humility cleanses *power-within* of its desire to be the center of attention, to focus the whole organization's efforts, decisions, and energy upon one heroic, charismatic leader. According to Matthew's Gospel, Jesus describes humility as an essential quality for discipleship. "Truly I tell you, unless you change and become like children, you will never enter the kingdom of heaven. Whoever becomes humble like this child is the greatest in the kingdom of heaven" (Matthew 18:3-4).

Those who lead with *power-within* sometimes use their gifts to promote their own importance. They believe they have a monopoly on spiritual gifts. These leaders feel empowered; but they effectively disempower others. Other members' gifts go underutilized and unnoticed. The leaders' need to be admired and flattered means that other people cannot develop their own God-given gifts. The effect of personal power and expertise can be to hypnotize people and dominate them. When this occurs, leaders do not have disciples; they have devotees.

Jesus steadfastly refuses to use his *power-within* in ways that make him the center of attention. He refuses to use his spiritual gifts to bedazzle and mesmerize. After Jesus' baptism, the Spirit leads him into the wilderness, where the devil puts him to the test. At one point, the devil tempts Jesus to throw himself from the pinnacle of the Temple, thus challenging Jesus to perform a miracle in order to draw attention to his powers and giftedness. Jesus rejects this temptation. He refuses to use his spiritual gifts for ministry to make himself the center of everyone's attention (Luke 4:9-12). He instead chooses the path of humble service that leads to the cross. Jesus rejects the path of a heroic leader who uses his charisma and expertise to dazzle, to mesmerize, to be the focus of everyone's hopes and desires.

Throughout his ministry, Jesus criticizes people who engage in religious practices primarily to draw people's attention to their own devotion or charisma. These people pray on the street corners where others can admire them. They give alms before the crowds so that others can praise their generosity. They cover themselves with sackcloth and ashes so that others know they are fasting.

Jesus sets humble service over against making oneself the focus of everyone's adulation and admiration.

> They do all their deeds to be seen by others. . . . They love to have the place of honor at banquets and the best seats in the synagogues, and to be greeted with respect in the marketplaces, and to have people call them rabbi. But you are not to be called rabbi, for you have one teacher, and you are all students. And call no one your father on earth, for you have one Father—the one in heaven. Nor are you to be called instructors, for you have one instructor, the Messiah. The greatest among you will be your servant. All who exalt themselves will be humbled, and all who humble themselves will be exalted. (Matthew 23:5-12)

Scholars have traditionally drawn attention to Mark's emphasis on Jesus' messianic secret. Whenever he heals someone, Jesus charges that person to remain silent about what he has done. After Jesus heals a little girl, for example, he "strictly ordered them that no one should know this" (Mark 5:43). Matthew records that Jesus ordered the disciples who had seen him transfigured on the mountaintop to keep silent about their experience (Matthew 17:9).

HUMBLE SERVICE AS AN INVITATION FOR OTHERS TO DISCOVER THEIR GIFTS

Rather than draw attention to himself, Jesus focuses people's attention on God's action in their lives. Jesus uses his *power-within* to invite others to discover their own spiritual gifts for ministry, not to admire his spiritual prowess.

When a woman in a crowd cries out, "Blessed is the womb that bore you and the breasts that nursed you," drawing attention to Jesus' special charisma, Jesus refuses to allow her to make him the focus of attention. He instead redirects the crowd's attention to God's activity in their midst: "But he said, 'Blessed rather are those who hear the word of God and obey it!'" (Luke 11:27-28). Jesus' sense of servanthood leads to a measured humility about his own importance. Jesus the Servant draws attention not to himself but to the One who sends him and to the community in which God is acting.

Jesus does not insist upon monopolizing all ministry. He empowers his disciples for ministry, sending them forth two-by-two to preach and heal. He does not claim that he is the only one with spiritual gifts. He affirms that whatever he does, his disciples can also do. After he heals the man named Legion, Jesus refuses to allow him to engage in hero-worship. Jesus insists that he remain in his own community and become a leader rather than a perpetual camp-follower. "And he went away and began to proclaim in the Decapolis how much Jesus had done for him; and everyone was amazed" (Mark 5:20).

Jesus as a servant leader generates abundance. He does not make people feel that they have nothing to offer and must rely on his charismatic gifts. He does not restrict certain ministries to himself. He does not treat ministry as a special possession that only he may perform. Servant leaders announce the abundance of *power-within*. They multiply power, inviting others into the circle of influence and reciprocity. They humbly acknowledge that they are not the only ones to whom God has given spiritual gifts for ministry.

Paul's letters and other early church documents suggest that humility was one of Jesus' most defining characteristics. Paul's letter to the Philippians urges two powerful women, who both possess *power-within*, to take Jesus' humility as their model for leading with power (Philippians 4:2–3; also 1:27–2:11). Peter urges his readers to have a tender heart and a humble mind (1 Peter 3:8). A little later, Peter tells people to "humble your-selves therefore under the mighty hand of God, so that he may exalt you in due time" (1 Peter 5:6).

These New Testament writers are not describing a false humility that has too often been used to oppress women and marginalize minorities. Such groups were told to be humble, meaning that they were to keep quiet and do as they were told. They obviously did not have anything important to share with those who wielded real power.

True humility does not disempower. It invites and empow-ers. It augments the authority of people's own experiences. It does not keep people on the sidelines, looking at what a soli-tary, heroic leader is doing for God. Jesus uses his charismatic power to inspire his followers. He does not use his personal magnetism to dominate them. He energizes, educates, and empowers his disciples.

It is unrealistic to prohibit people who possess personal magnetism, charisma, and expertise from exercising their con-siderable *power-within*. The question is not whether leaders may legitimately use *power-within*. The more fundamental issue is how they use these special gifts for ministry. Do they use these gifts to mesmerize and bedazzle, to impress and domi-nate? Or do they use these gifts to inspire, to educate, to empower others?

Servanthood acts as a helpful guideline for distinguishing between these two expressions of *power-within*. Humble ser-vanthood reminds us that in all but the most rare occasions, one is too small a number to produce greatness.

JESUS' SERVANTHOOD AND *POWER-WITH*

The New Testament uses another Greek word besides *exousia* to describe Jesus' power. The Greek word *dunamis* occurs more than one-hundred times in the New Testament. *Dunamis* shares the same root meaning as the English words *dynamite* and *dynamic*. *Dunamis* suggests that the power with which Jesus leads is dynamic and fluid. It is not static and fixed. It is neither a commodity nor an inner resource. Power is dynamic because it flows from mutuality, collaboration, and interaction. *Dunamis* is *power-with*.

We often picture Jesus as alone on the cross. But the Gospels more frequently portray him as surrounded by companions and friends. He is at table-fellowship with tax collectors, sinners, and disciples. He has gathered a crowd around him and is teaching.

Jesus does not just dispense charity and alms to the marginalized. No one would have sought his crucifixion had he merely engaged in acts of mercy. Jesus, however, insisted on eating and drinking with the marginalized. He went beyond charity and good works. He shared power with the powerless.

Power-with is the experience of shared power. Friends and colleagues recognize that differences enrich the relationship. They do not all bring the same thing to the relationship. They do not all contribute equally. *Power-with* depends upon mutuality. The give-and-take of mutuality generates new energy and creativity. It expands power. Communion with Jesus generates abundance. In the feeding stories, Jesus turns fragmented resources and privately held goods into bountiful nourishment available to all people. Jesus leads in ways that weave a web of voluntary, mutual responsibility.

This generative, co-active understanding of power explains

why Jesus can perform no miracles in his hometown. When the townspeople in Jesus' home community refuse to enter into a relationship of mutuality, equality, and collaboration with him, he has no power to lead (Mark 6:1-6).

Jesus' ability to exercise *power-with*, on the other hand, never degenerates into exclusivism and elitism. Friendships with Jesus never turn in upon themselves. Jesus the Servant purifies *power-with* of its tendency to turn inward and to close itself off from the needs of the outside world. Jesus' parable of the good Samaritan (Luke 10:25-37) underscores how servanthood challenges friendship's tendency to curve in upon itself, thus excluding outsiders.

When the disciples turn the crowds away and refuse to allow children to touch Jesus, he rebukes them: "Let the little children come to me; do not stop them; for it is to such as these that the kingdom of God belongs. Truly I tell you, whoever does not receive the kingdom of God as a little child will never enter it" (Mark 10:14-15). When Peter, James, and John try to remain on the mountain after Jesus' transfiguration, offering to build booths where they might dwell apart from the world, Jesus firmly leads them back down the mountain (Matthew 17:1-8).

According to Mark's Gospel, Jesus invites his disciples to withdraw to a quiet place apart, where they might retreat and rest after their missionary journeys. They are tired and weary. They need time alone with one another. But the crowds follow Jesus to this deserted place. The disciples want to send them away, particularly when they discover that they have nothing to feed these people. Jesus refuses to let the disciples circle the wagons, turn inward upon themselves, and forget the needs of the world. He calls them to be servants, to feed the hungry crowds. And they discover that despite what appears to be minimal resources, they have more than enough to meet both their needs and the world's (Mark 6:30-44).

Even Jesus himself struggles with the temptation to exclusivity. When he travels to Tyre and Sidon, a Canaanite woman comes out and begs him to heal her child. At first, Jesus refuses. After all, she is a Canaanite and he is Jewish. Why "take the children's food and throw it to the dogs"? Yet the woman confronts Jesus and challenges him to widen his circle of compassion (Matthew 15:21-28).

I tend to believe that leaders work best when they exercise *power-with*. As I said earlier, at one time in my life I thought *power-with* was the only legitimate way for leaders to exercise power. Yet I have tempered my enthusiasm for *power-with*. I have come to realize that despite its great strengths, even *power-with* can have negative consequences. It can degenerate into exclusivism. It can turn inward and become comfortable with a cocoon of close friends.

THE COMMUNITY OF THE BELOVED DISCIPLE AND THE DANGERS OF *POWER-WITH*

The traditions behind John's Gospel and letters reveal both the strength of *power-with* and its inherent weaknesses.[4] For John's Gospel, loving relationships lie at the center of Christian life. John 10:1-11 portrays Jesus as the model shepherd, not because he has a position of authority or special gifts but because he has intimate knowledge of the sheep and loves them. Similarly, in John 21, Jesus tells Peter to tend his sheep. Before this bestowal of authority, however, Jesus asks Peter three times, "Do you love me?" Love and friendship—not spiritual gifts, not positional power—are the criteria for faithful leadership in the Johannine community.

In the same way, the term *apostle* is completely absent from all the Johannine writings, both the Gospel and the letters. No single heroic apostle is emphasized as in the Pauline tradition (as reflected in Paul's letters and the Pastoral Epistles) or in the Petrine tradition (as found in sources like Mark's Gospel). Instead, John focuses on the beloved disciple. This figure is the disciple whom Jesus loved most. Love and friendship—not spiritual gifts, not hierarchical office—are the keys to faithful discipleship.

This is a profoundly egalitarian vision of Christian community. There are no apostles who hold official positions. No heroic, charismatic leaders dominate the community. Instead we have a beloved community of friends. This community generates *power-with*. In its midst is life abundant.

By the time of the Johannine letters, however, this intimate friendship has given way to a nasty hostility toward outsiders. John's Gospel itself does not seem to emphasize love of the neighbor, only love of one's fellow companions in faith. The letters themselves now go beyond indifference to the neighbor. They express outright hostility. The outsider is a threat, an enemy. The Second Letter of John begins with an invitation for the author and recipient to love each other, for God is love. It then immediately shifts to a condemnation of all who do not share in this close community of love. These outsiders are deceivers (2 John 7). They are not to be received as guests to whom hospitality is extended (2 John 10). Everything is depicted in sharp contrasts of light and darkness, good and evil, love and hate.

WHOM DO WE SERVE?

Without the counterbalance of servanthood, *power-with* can stray into an inwardly focused exclusivity. Friends can care deeply about one another while remaining completely indifferent to the needs of others around them. The mark of a friendly church is ultimately not how much members care for one another; it is how well they serve the stranger. Too often we remain content in comfortable enclaves where everyone is like us. Jesus the Servant calls us to move beyond comfortable intimacy and to serve the same marginalized, invisible people that he invited to his table fellowship.

Servanthood acts as a benchmark by which we judge the faithfulness of *power-with*. Does our Christian fellowship issue in service to the marginalized and excluded? Does it result in ministry that serves the forgotten ones for whom Christ came, died, and rose again? Jesus the Servant calls us to ministries of service: "For I was hungry and you gave me food, I was thirsty and you gave me something to drink, I was a stranger and you welcomed me, I was naked and you gave me clothing, I was sick and you took care of me, I was in prison and you visited me" (Matthew 25:35-36).

QUESTIONS FOR LEADERS

Jesus' own ministry demonstrates that there is no single best way to lead with power. Jesus' own exercise of the power to lead reminds us that people can be faithful leaders whether they exercise *power-over*, *power-within*, or *power-with*. The leader's faithfulness depends not on the type of power being wielded but on the spirit of servanthood that infuses and undergirds it. Servanthood transforms the power to lead into faithful leadership that is a dynamic relationship between partners in the gospel who intend real changes that reflect commonly-held purposes.

Faithful leaders ask themselves the following questions:

• When I exercise *power-over*, do I have as my ultimate aim a time when we will be equal partners, regardless of any inequality that now exists between us? Or am I leading in ways that preserve inequality and insure my status or authority?

• When I exercise *power-over*, am I acting on behalf of common values and shared purposes that unite everyone concerned? Or am I acting on my own behalf? Am I serving myself or serving our shared purposes? Who benefits from my leading? Who pays?

• When I exercise *power-within*, am I aware of how my behavior affects others around me? Am I making them dependent upon me or fostering their growth and independence? Am I empowering or disempowering them? Do I use my gifts and expertise to make others serve me and my needs or to further Christ's ministry of service in the world?

• When I exercise *power-within*, am I using my gifts or expertise to dazzle and hypnotize others, impressing them with my abilities? Or am I using my gifts and expertise to educate, to empower, to encourage? Am I acting in ways that serve others or that encourage others to serve me?

• When I exercise *power-within*, am I keeping everyone's attention on me so that I remain the center of community life? Or am I drawing out other people's gifts, encouraging them to play a more active role?

• When I exercise *power-with*, am I unintentionally allowing the community to turn inward? Or am I mobilizing their resources to be in ministry to the larger world?

QUESTIONS FOR REFLECTION

1. Can you describe some situations in which servanthood has redeemed the exercise of *power-over*?
2. Can you describe some situations in which servanthood has purified the exercise of *power-within*?
3. Can you describe some situations in which servant-leaders have helped Christian communities refocus their energy

from exclusion and elitism to service and ministry?

4. The text lists six guidelines (pages 73–74) for how servant-hood prevents the abuse of power. Can you think of additional guidelines?

Partners in the Gospel

Christianity is ultimately a social religion, not a solitary one. We cannot be Christians by ourselves. We are Christians only as we participate in Christian communities of faith. Baptism, Christianity's rite of initiation, signals its social character. We do not baptize ourselves. It takes two or more people to baptize. One administers the water; the second receives it. We never "do baptism" alone. We do it together as a community.

In the same way, individuals never "do leadership." Individuals may lead with power, but leadership happens within a community. Leadership happens when mutual service transforms individuals who lead with power into partners in the gospel who share in leadership. Leadership is a social practice. Mutuality, service, and collaboration are the seedbed in which it thrives.

This social, relational understanding of leadership should come naturally to most Christians, given Christianity's social nature. Unfortunately, the collaborative partnerships that give rise to leadership do not come naturally to most North American Christians.

OUR CULTURE TEACHES COMPETITION, NOT COLLABORATION

Our two sons, Robert and Jonathan, love board games. Most of these games teach competition. One player wins. The others lose. One player collects all the money. The others go bankrupt. As I play a board game with my children, I feel the tension rising as one player comes closer to winning.

EDUCATION FOR COMPETITION

Games are not the only place where children learn to compete. Our whole educational system orients us to competition rather than collaboration. Teachers grade their tests on a bell curve. A few students receive A's. Most get C's. For every winner, many are losers. When children do collaborate on the answers, the teacher labels it as cheating and punishes those involved.

Our schools' explicit curricula also bias us against collaborative partnerships. Textbooks present history as a series of accomplishments by great individuals. War and conflict emerge out of competition for scarce resources. Nations and great leaders compete for power and glory.

Teachers explain science as the work of solitary geniuses working alone in their laboratories, yet we know that science is intensely collaborative. The truly great scientific breakthroughs occur because researchers work together. It took the collaborative community of Bohr, Heisenberg, and others to discover quantum physics. Science is less the dramatic breakthrough of a lone researcher in his or her laboratory than the patient work of collaborative communities working across space and time.

We teach music and art as if isolated creators struggle alone in their studios and garrets. Yet even artistic advancement usually emerges from collaboration and partnership. The Impressionists, for example, worked as a collaborative community. In their early years, Monet and Renoir set their easels side-by-side and worked as partners.

Society organizes its schools to reflect the world of work. Work environments are usually structured to reward solitary effort rather than partnership and collaboration. We reward the "outstanding employee of the month." Seldom do companies recognize the "outstanding team of the year." Compensation is based on individual performance, not the team's output.

Partnership and collaboration do not come naturally, especially in our North American culture. Being a good partner requires effort and training.

WE LACK TOOLS FOR PARTNERSHIP AND COLLABORATION

No wonder we have such difficulties with leadership. We lack the concepts and tools needed for collaboration and partnership. Yet collaboration and partnership are the seedbed from which leadership grows.

We would never hand sheet music to musicians and expect them to play without instruments. We would never give carpenters lumber but no hammers and saws. No one believes that a doctor could work effectively if we provided an examining room but no thermometers, stethoscope, or other equipment. Yet we persist in believing that communities can have faithful leadership even though their members lack the necessary tools.

If we are to discover values and tools for collaboration, our best resource is the New Testament. Its authors present us with profound insights into how partnership and servanthood are the foundations for leadership.

LEADERSHIP, SERVICE, AND PARTNERSHIP

Leadership emerges from the dynamic interaction of service and partnership in Christian community. Luke observes that Peter, James, and John are partners (*koinonia*) in a common fishing enterprise. When Jesus calls them to be his disciples, he invites them into a new partnership (*koinonia*) in which they will now catch people rather than fish (Luke 5:1-11). *Koinonia* is a key concept in the New Testament. We normally translate this Greek word with the English term *fellowship*, which usually connotes warm-fuzzy intimacy. It suggests interpersonal closeness and a cocoon-like community surrounding us.

Yet *koinonia* has a far richer meaning. Only rarely in the New Testament does *koinonia* mean friendly sharing and caring. More typically it refers to partnerships in which people are drawn together around a common project or purpose. Each partner contributes something to the relationship. Each receives something from it. Service to shared purposes is the glue that binds partners together.[5]

PAULINE PARTNERSHIPS IN CHRIST

Paul frequently describes his mission as a partnership. Leadership in the early Pauline churches stems from this fundamental partnership in service to God's mission and ministry. Paul and his churches are partners with God in a common project already inaugurated by God in Jesus Christ. When James, Peter, and John extend the "right hand of fellowship" (*koinonia*) to Paul and Barnabas at the Jerusalem Council, all parties are agreeing on a common, binding obligation (Galatians 2:9). All are agreeing to a common service in the name of Jesus. Some will extend this service to the Jews; others, to the Gentiles. The right hand of fellowship is not a warm welcome into an enclave of like-minded individuals. It comes closer to being the handshake that seals a business deal.

Paul reminds the Philippians that they share in a partnership (*koinonia*) in the gospel (Philippians 1:5). They are partners with Paul and God in a common project of continuing Jesus' service to God's divine project in the world. Each partner has something to give and something to receive (Philippians 4:15). A three-way partnership exists. The collaborative relationship between Paul and the Philippians is really a partnership initiated in and continued by God. Paul playfully describes God as an accountant, keeping the partnership's books:

> Not that I seek the gift, but I seek the profit that accumulates to your account. I have been paid in full and have more than enough; I am fully satisfied . . . And my God will fully satisfy every need of yours according to his riches in glory in Christ Jesus.
> (Philippians 4:17-19)

Paul reminds his Philippian readers of this three-way partnership just before his hymn to Christ the Servant:

> If then there is any encouragement in Christ, any consolation from love, any sharing [*koinonia*] in the Spirit, any compassion and sympathy, make my joy complete: be of the same mind, having the same love, being in full accord and of one mind. . . . Let each of you look not to your own interests, but to the interests of others. Let the same mind be in you that was in Christ Jesus. (Philippians 2:1-2,4)

Paul here draws together the three themes we are considering: service, partnership, and leadership. Paul, the Philippians, and Jesus Christ are partners in a common mission of humble service. Leadership for the Philippian church emerges from this partnership in serving the world.

SERVANTHOOD AND PARTNERSHIP ARE THE SEEDBED FOR LEADERSHIP

Perhaps this language of partnership, service, and leadership developed out of Paul's conversations with early converts such as Lydia, who was obviously a shrewd businesswoman. When he writes to the Corinthians, Paul refers to his partnership with the Philippian church. "We want you to know, brothers and sisters, about the grace of God that has been granted to the churches of Macedonia," Paul begins (2 Corinthians 8:1). The Philippians begged "earnestly for the privilege of sharing [koinonia] in this ministry to the saints—and this, not merely as we expected; they gave themselves first to the Lord and, by the will of God, to us" (8:4-5). Drawn into a relationship with God in Christ, the Philippians become collaborators with Paul. A three-way partnership emerges between God, Paul, and the Philippians.

Leadership occurs as an overflow of this relationship of mutuality, reciprocity, and service among partners in the gospel. Thus Paul reminds the Corinthians that Titus's role of leader derives from this shared partnership in Christ. "We might urge Titus that, as he had already made a beginning, so he should also complete this generous undertaking among you" (2 Corinthians 8:6).

Partnerships have no room for domination, manipulation, and coercion. They leave no place for attempts to bedazzle, hypnotize, and mesmerize. They have room only for servants who value mutuality, reciprocity, and communion. Paul uses partnership language to encourage—but not command— Philemon to receive Onesimus as a brother instead of as a slave. "So if you consider me your partner [koinonia], welcome him as you would welcome me" (Philemon 17).

Similarly, in his letter to the Romans, Paul initially announces that he is coming to give them things they lack. Practically catching himself in mid-sentence, however, he immediately shifts his tone. He reminds both his readers and himself that he comes as a partner in Christ who will receive as well as give: "For I am longing to see you so that I may share with you some spiritual gift to strengthen you—or rather so that we may be mutually encouraged by each other's faith, both yours and mine" (Romans 1:11-12).

No individual may lord it over others. Rather, all participate in relationships of mutuality, equality, and service. Paul serves the Romans by bringing insights and gifts to them. They, in turn, serve Paul by encouraging his faith. Leadership evolves out of these dynamic relationships of service among partners in the gospel.

Partnership is the context for service. And, paradoxically, service is also the context for partnership. There is no service, from Paul's perspective, without partnership. God serves humankind because God has chosen to be our covenant partner. We serve because God has reached out in Jesus Christ and made us partners with him in witness, mission, and service. Conversely, there is no partnership without service. Partnerships are formed for the purpose of service. God in Christ becomes our partner in order that service may occur. One cannot exist without the other.

Leadership acquires its own particular shape as it emerges from this interaction between partnership and service. Because it involves partnership, leadership is relational. Collaboration, not domination, becomes the standard of excellence. Because it involves service, leadership has service—not subordination—as its purpose. Partners, by definition, cannot be competitors. They are collaborators engaged in common service.

WHAT IS COLLABORATION?

We may be tempted to define collaboration as treating people like pieces of a jigsaw puzzle. The leader fits all the pieces together to achieve his or her grand vision. Sometimes we use words like *cooperation* and *collaboration* as another way of saying that we expect people to do what we want them to do.

COMMUNICATION IS NOT COLLABORATION

I am trying to hurry out the door and my sons are dawdling over their boots and coats. They are getting ready to leave on their own timetable, not mine. So I blurt out, "Let's have some cooperation around here." What I really mean is, "Do what I tell you." In the same way, a leader can talk about collaboration. But what he or she really means is that everyone should work together to do what the leader wants accomplished. Partners, however, are not pieces of a jigsaw puzzle. They are not preengineered patterns that can be plugged into someone else's predetermined design.

What, then, do we mean by collaboration? Like many other concepts, we can more easily describe what collaboration is *not* than define what it is. First, collaboration is not always the same as groupwork. Groups can be little more than the sum of individual actions. Such groups come together and discuss what each member is doing. Information is distributed. Then each member goes back to his or her solitary work. Collaboration is not the same as sharing information so that group members know what everyone is individually working on. After all, people can work side-by-side without being willing or able to collaborate as partners with a common purpose.

COLLABORATION IS CO-CREATION OF MEANING AND PURPOSE

Collaborative partnerships do not require more communication. They demand a particular quality of interaction. Displaying knowledge or skill is less important than creating a *shared space* where everyone creates new knowledge and hones new skills.

Collaboration is the process of shared creation. Partners with complementary skills interact to generate new visions, new understandings, new ways of being and doing.

COLLABORATION AND GOD'S CALCULATED INEFFICIENCY

Collaboration involves partners who know that they cannot achieve truly important purposes by themselves. Leadership emerges out of this creative exchange in which people construct a common purpose and shared vision. Each partner can lead with power only so long as he or she allows space for others to share their gifts and to exercise their power.

Leadership thus involves a calculated inefficiency. The necessary gifts and resources are widely and unequally distributed. The key resource is usually hidden in the least likely member of the congregation. The crucial insight may reside in the person whose views we barely tolerate. Leaders who need to dominate others cannot embrace leadership's calculated inefficiency. Neither can the powerful personality who needs to bedazzle others or who finds it so much easier to do everything himself or herself.

Yet God is seldom efficient. God frequently chooses the least likely candidate for a task. Moses was a fugitive. David was a shepherd and a youngest son. Peter was brash. Paul was a persecutor of the church. Partnership reminds us that everyone— especially the weakest, the least likely, the most marginalized—

has gifts to share. All have services to render if we serve them by creating a hospitable space where they may flourish. Mutual service in Christ's name honors God's calculated inefficiency. Partners in the gospel seek out the marginalized member's opinion. They treat unpopular viewpoints with respect. They protect the voices of those without formal authority in the congregation. Mutual service creates a space where all may flourish and blossom.

COLLABORATION REQUIRES SHARED SPACES

Meetings are the formal structures for collaboration in most congregations. Unfortunately, many meetings are ineffective vehicles for collaboration. Participants do not create a shared understanding. They do not create a larger purpose that unites partners in common service. Consider this all-too-common example: Some members of Good Shepherd Church's education committee come late to the meeting. Others leave early. Usually they are present in time to share information related to their particular item on the agenda. They then excuse themselves. One member quietly grades her sixth graders' book reports, half listening to items that do not pertain directly to her. The chairperson may not have a written agenda. While the room has a dry-erase board hanging on one wall, no one uses it to record comments, keep track of decisions, or list issues as they surface. Committee members are expected to keep track of the discussion in their own heads. Everyone keeps his or her own private record of actions taken and decisions made. Because members sometimes have different assumptions about what has been decided, these private records may vary significantly.

The potential for leadership is thus undermined in the very setting where it should thrive. Fortunately, church members can take some simple steps to improve meetings as collaborative environments where leadership can emerge.[6]

First, partnerships need more than tables and chairs for their meeting space. They also require newsprint, a dry-erase board, or a chalkboard. They need a shared space where thoughts, ideas, facts, questions, and disagreements can be recorded. Newsprint, dry-erase boards, or chalkboards are the most pervasive collaborative media. When participants work with a group product using one of these media, they shift from planning or reviewing work to actually doing work. Creating a tangible product together shifts the emphasis from passive listening to active construction.

Newsprint, dry-erase boards, or chalkboards are also helpful for recording important ideas and images from conversations. Conversations do not have memories; only participants do. Consequently, participants in a meeting usually respond to what has just been said, not to something said a few minutes earlier. They have already forgotten those earlier comments. Conversation's serial, ephemeral nature works against collaboration and thus undercuts leadership.

In most conversations, the absence of memory means that a useful phrase, insight, or suggestion can be forgotten, lost, or distorted. In ordinary conversations, words are like soap bubbles. They float around, evoke some response, then pop and disappear. But in a collaborative environment, ideas and images can be preserved on the shared space of a dry-erase board, chalkboard, or newsprint. Participants can refer back to the ideas, play with them, recombine them, or alter them.

The board or newsprint becomes a shared space where partners collaborate. Shared space adds a new dimension to the conversation, a dimension of memory, symbolic representation, and creativity. Ideas put into shared space can be expanded, organized, altered, merged, clarified, and otherwise reshaped until they generate totally new meanings. It takes shared space to create shared meanings and shared purposes. These shared purposes unite partners in common service. Leadership flows from this common service among partners.

Shared spaces such as dry-erase boards and newsprint have some common characteristics. First, they make it easy to move ideas or images around and tinker with them. Second, they provoke the senses as well as the mind. Participants see words, smell the marker's ink, touch the rough paper or smooth board surface, or feel the chalk dust. Shared spaces involve the whole person and not just the mind. Third, shared spaces work asynchronously. That is, participants can return to ideas left on newsprint several minutes—or even several hours—ago. Participants can leave notes and ideas for other team members to read later, long after they have left. Fourth, participants can easily play in shared space. Dissimilar elements can be combined. Images can be reworked. Playful combinations can emerge. Fifth, shared spaces heal the rift between visual and verbal language. A picture is worth a thousand words, yet too often we settle for words, not pictures. We can visualize our future on a board or paper, drawing a picture rather than just talking about it.

Our office has a large four-by-six dry-erase board hung along one whole wall. Everyone on our team uses this dry-erase board to record thoughts and ideas. We list projects and timelines. We check off when something is done. We draw a bell around something that alarms us. The six of us come and go. We are all busy with different responsibilities, yet the dry-erase board serves as shared space, reminding us that we are partners in a common project.

The dry-erase board helps us see the larger picture. It allows us to represent visually what we are working to achieve. Even when we do not have time to speak with one another, we communicate through the dry-erase board. The dry-erase board is a shared space that helps us build a collaborative partnership. Equally important, this shared space plays a crucial role in generating leadership. It sometimes seems that the dry-erase board itself is our team leader. Its timelines and messages keep us honest and motivate us. They remind us of key tasks and prod us to do better. I cease to be the team leader who gives orders to subordinates. Rather, the staff and I together exercise leadership through our partnership symbolized on our dry-erase board.

In some homes I have seen a similar phenomenon. Somewhere—often near the door or telephone—is a chalkboard or dry-erase board where family members leave messages and communicate asynchronously. This board is a shared space. It unites and binds together the family members.

I try to bring newsprint to most meetings. Some people poke fun at me, asking if I own stock in paper companies. They ask if I am addicted to the smell of magic markers. Yet both they and I realize how the newsprint fosters partnership, collaboration, and leadership. Ideas that emerge from our conversations are recorded on the newsprint. We can return to these ideas, add new thoughts, alter them, or recombine them in novel ways. As we work together within this shared space, we become partners—not just individuals with separate responsibilities who have come together to report what we are doing.

I have seen enormous creativity emerge from a planning retreat as a group builds its thoughts and ideas over a few hours or days, recording their reflections on a shared space of newsprint. As the walls are plastered with paper, participants begin to make connections, to see new possibilities, to create a shared vision. The data on the newsprint no longer belongs to any one person who may have initially spoken his or her thoughts. It belongs to the group. Because the group owns this data, it becomes powerful and generative.

Shared spaces help convert each participant's power to lead into a commonly shared leadership that arises from within the group. As participants become partners, new energy is released. Servant leaders are less concerned about people accepting their ideas and opinions than about helping groups grow beyond their current understandings and discover new purposes that inspire and empower.

COLLABORATIVE ENVIRONMENTS AND POWER

When we work in collaborative environments, we experience the dynamic flow of power in particular ways. Collaborative environments and shared spaces hold in check the negative aspects of power.

Collaborative environments still require individuals who occupy official positions and exercise positional *power-over*. Yet, precisely because collaborative environments value equality and mutuality, *power-over*'s tendency to dominate and manipulate is eliminated. All participants perceive themselves as equals, regardless of temporary differences in power between them. Collaborative environments keep the group's shared purposes in the forefront of participants' thinking and acting. This emphasis on shared purposes diminishes the temptation to use positional power to achieve one's own personal ends.

Collaborative environments value all participants' gifts and contributions. Everyone has something to share in a collaborative environment. Hence, it is more difficult for those with special expertise or charisma to make themselves the center of everyone's attention. Shared spaces place a premium on participation and involvement. Consequently, participants seek ways to strengthen and empower—rather than to disempower—one another. Shared spaces thus militate against the worst abuses of *power-within*.

Finally, collaborative environments actively embody the values of *power-with*. Shared spaces emphasize mutuality, relationship, and interaction. Because collaborative environments usually focus on goal-oriented projects, they are less likely to degenerate into a warm intimacy that excludes others. We create shared spaces in order to work on commonly acknowledged challenges and opportunities, not to engage in interpersonal closeness for its own sake.

Collaborative environments thus generate relationships and dynamics that encourage the positive expression of *power-over*, *power-within*, and *power-with*. In these environments, mutual service and servant leadership can thrive and flourish.

QUESTIONS FOR REFLECTION

1. Describe some examples of how you have been programmed by our society to compete rather than to collaborate.
2. What feelings do you have when you feel that you are competing with others for a scarce reward or honor? How do you feel about yourself? about others?
3. What are some times and places in which you learned to collaborate? What were these experiences like for you? What did you learn from these experiences?
4. This chapter describes the importance of shared spaces in partnership and leadership. Besides using dry-erase boards, chalkboards, and newsprint, can you think of other ways we create shared spaces?
5. Can you describe a time when a shared space played a significant role in a group that you were a part of? What

happened? What was the experience like for you and others?

6. What are some ways you might use shared spaces in your efforts to collaborate with others? Can you be a servant to the group by helping them develop shared spaces?

Chapter Five

Forthright & Listening Leadership

C ollaboration requires more than just shared spaces. Collaborative leadership requires that partners know how to balance advocacy of their own ideas with an ability to inquire into how others are construing the same situation. They must balance advocacy with inquiry.[7] They must be forthright in expressing their own views, yet they must also be able to listen to how others perceive the situation. They become servants to their conversation partners, helping them better understand and better state their own opinions.

BALANCING ADVOCACY WITH INQUIRY

Most of us do not know how to balance advocacy with inquiry. We instead utilize a "mystery-mastery" model to deal with people. First, we assume that someone else is responsible when we encounter a problem. Second, we develop a private explanation for what the other person is doing wrong. But we never share our opinion with anyone else, especially not the individual concerned. Then, based on our diagnosis of what the other person is doing wrong, we try to get him or her to change. When the other person does not respond to our suggestions, we interpret this as a confirmation that we are right and they are wrong. Finally, the more they resist us, the more we view them as totally responsible for the problem.

This mystery-mastery approach assumes competition and conflict between people. It leaves no room for collaboration and partnership. The mystery-mastery model thus fits perfectly with the charismatic leader who wants to mesmerize others. It is well-suited for the expert leader who seeks to bedazzle the community. When leaders with positional power drift into the mystery-mastery model, they end up manipulating or coercing others.

Servant leaders, on the other hand, attempt to balance advocacy with inquiry. When they encounter a problem or challenge, they still develop a diagnosis and prescription. But instead of keeping this perspective private, they share it with their collaborators. They publicly advocate for their perspective. Equally important, they inquire into how others are construing the situation. They listen to other perspectives. They balance advocacy of their own perspective with inquiry into why others see the situation differently. They know how to be forthright about their opinions; yet they balance their forthrightness with a willingness to listen to others.

If we place advocacy and inquiry on a grid, we end up with at least four possible balances of advocacy and inquiry (see Figure 2, page 95). Partners can be low on both advocacy and inquiry. When this happens, partnership becomes impossible. If I neither share what I think nor listen to what you think, no relationship exists between us. Yet relationships are the seedbed from which generative leadership emerges.

Partners can also be high on advocacy but low on inquiry. In this case, partnership also ceases to exist. Collaboration is replaced by domination. Mutuality and reciprocity give way to competition and one-way influence. Trinity Church's lay leader, Sally Mitchell, is constantly talking. She has an opinion about everyone and everything—usually an unfavorable one. Every meeting is a soapbox onto which Sally climbs, an opportunity to tell everyone what she thinks. Sally thinks she is exercising leadership. Indeed, many of Trinity Church's members also think Sally is exerting leadership. Some of them consequently avoid becoming leaders. They do not want to be like Sally. Yet Sally is not exerting faithful leadership. She is high on advocacy but fails to inquire into other people's values, views, and perspectives. She cannot treat others as equal partners in a relationship of mutuality, reciprocity, and sharing.

As a third alternative, partners can be high on inquiry but low on advocacy. They spend their time asking questions about what others think, but they never reveal what they believe. Other people experience them as a blank slate. No one knows what they think or feel. Once again, faithful leadership cannot emerge under such conditions. Leadership grows out of relationships. If one party in the relationship withholds information, feelings, thoughts, or opinions, then a genuine relationship cannot exist. Leadership as a relationship of mutual influence among partners cannot exist when people are unwilling to share their feelings and thoughts.

Figure 2

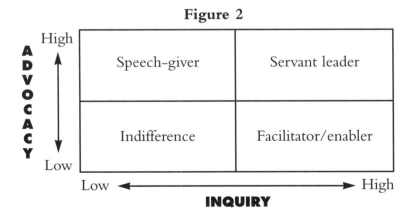

Martino Hernandez wonders why his congregation is slowly declining. Martino is an effective listener. He asks questions, draws others out. Pastors in his district often invite him to assist with their churchwide planning retreats. They admire his skill as a facilitator. Yet no one ever knows what Martino himself thinks. When the congregation was deciding whether to allow a community group to move into an unused section of the education building, members asked Martino what he thought. Martino responded, "It's not important what I think. I'm here only to help you make decisions about your church." Martino was a terminal facilitator. Members expected Martino to lead. They wanted him to assist them in thinking theologically about their choices. But he refused to enter into this arena with them. Members cannot have a relationship with someone who never shares his or her thoughts, feelings, hopes, fears, dreams. Trying to have a relationship with Martino is a one-way street. He remains a distant, somewhat indifferent figure.

Faithful leadership develops where leaders have the capacity to both advocate and inquire, the fourth possibility. When leaders are high on both advocacy and inquiry, faithful leadership occurs within a group. "I create fair and open processes," remarked Michelle Bahary, "because I want to make sure my ideas get a fair hearing along with everyone else's." Michelle knew how to advocate for her views, but she wanted to understand what others thought as well. She knew how to engage Christ Church's members in a dialogue about the challenges that faced them. "I believe in a public church," Michelle continued. "I mean public in two ways. The whole congregation is involved, and all the information is out there where we can all look at it. Nothing's privately held. Secrets are enormously destructive."

Everyone has part of the truth on his or her own. No one

has all of it. We only discover the whole truth by speaking forthrightly and listening openly to one another.

THE IMPORTANCE OF A GROUP'S LIFE CYCLE

Servant leadership cannot be willed into existence overnight. It develops over time. It has a particular life cycle that must be honored and that we must work with.[8] As mutual service between group members grows and deepens, the group generates different types of leadership. Leaders who confuse their power to lead with the group's leadership often disregard the group's developmental needs. They thus undermine their exercise of leadership.

During the *forming stage* of a ministry team or work group, its members are getting to know one another. The basic question is whether they will be in or out of the group. Participants size one another up and ask themselves if they really want to be partners with these people. Team members are most dependent upon their leader during this stage. They look to the designated leader to provide information about the team's goals and purposes. They expect the designated leader to model for them what behaviors are appropriate to this group and to orient them to team norms and values.

Those who lead with *power-over*, particularly those appointed as the group's convener or designated leader, have a critical role to play during this stage. They cannot abdicate their power to lead and become just another member of the group. They cannot become a terminal facilitator when the group needs someone with positional power to model appropriate behavior and set boundaries on the team's task.

During the *storming stage*, the team struggles to establish leadership and direction. *Storming* implies open, hostile conflict;

but this type of conflict does not always occur. Working through this stage can sometimes occur more calmly and quietly. Conflict happens along two fronts during this stage. First, team members may experience conflict among themselves. Second, conflict can emerge between the designated leader and team members. The key issue for the team is whether members feel "up" or "down." They ask, *What kind of power do I have to influence the team?*

Partners must be willing to share publicly their expectations of the group and to negotiate realistic expectations for what can be accomplished. They must also be willing to give up any unrealistic expectations about what the designated leader can accomplish for them. As team members negotiate these differences, they become partners. Their interactions become the seedbed from which servant leadership emerges.

Leaders who rely on *power-over* feel a need to dominate the group. Leaders who depend on *power-within* want to impress the group with their expertise or to capture it with their forceful personality. Precisely because they have these tendencies, such leaders often have difficulty negotiating this stage in the team's development. They want to hold on to their special role rather than let mutuality and reciprocity develop within the group. They remain "the leader," but leadership fails to develop. Not willing to let go of their special status, they stunt the team's development. Partnership withers and fades away. Participants refuse to become servants to one another and the group. Members never move beyond their own assertions of power to discover the dynamics of genuine leadership.

When team members and their leaders are aware of this stage's crucial tasks, they are better able to negotiate its difficult transitions. Servant leadership is difficult to achieve unless the team passes through a period in which leadership is experienced as emerging from the group. Servant leadership cannot thrive until individual members begin to give up their unrealistic expectations and instead begin co-constructing common purposes that are larger than any privately held, individual expectation they brought.

The *norming stage* involves development of stable patterns that characterize the team's life. Roles within the group develop and become more fixed. Certain people assume responsibility for particular tasks. An established framework begins to appear and guide participants' interactions. The team knows how to manage their meetings.

Some common complaints about meetings that can be addressed during this stage are (1) the lack of an agenda to guide conversations; (2) the length of time the team will meet; (3) situations in which issues are raised but never resolved; (4) situations in which action items are agreed upon but team members are not held accountable for follow-through; (5) time-wasters and unfocused discussions.

Hope Church holds an annual orientation and organizational meeting for its committees and administrative board every January. During worship, committee and board members are recognized and installed. A church potluck luncheon follows worship. Once the tables are cleared, members have a time of general orientation to leader skills.

Finally, they break into their individual councils, committees, and boards. Each ministry team reviews the group norms they had developed the previous year. New members are invited to revise these lists. Members covenant together to honor them. Most teams keep their norms on newsprint and post them at their meetings. The norms remind team members of their common commitments to one another. Power to enforce the norms does not lie with a single leader who dominates the team. The power of enforcement lies within the group as a whole. Leadership derives from the relational dynamics between team members.

The *performing stage* represents the generative work of the team. Team members have become servants and partners who engage in co-creation with one another. Leadership emerges from the group's relational dynamics. Collaboration, mutuality, equality, and service characterize the team's life.

Group members and leaders need to understand the varying leadership needs of these four stages. Consider, for example, the forming and storming stages. Members are not threatened by the authority of a designated leader as a new team forms. Similarly, the designated leader needs to understand that it is irresponsible merely to be a facilitator or just another member of the group during the forming stage. New groups depend upon the designated leader to provide direction and guidance.

During the storming stage, leaders and followers understand that dissonance or even conflict are essential to the team's development. Without this dissonance, they will never become partners. Until they become partners, they cannot experience the power of leadership. Leaders face a particular challenge during this stage. They sometimes have difficulty letting go of control or attention, thus stunting the team's developing partnership. Or their fear of conflict causes them to quash any voicing of differences and dissonance.

TRINITY, PARTNERSHIP, AND LEADERSHIP

On the wall beside our kitchen table, we have a copy of Rublev's icon of the Holy Trinity. Three angels, representing the three strangers who visited Abraham and Sarah (Genesis 18), are seated around a table. These three angels signify the three persons of the Trinity. The three angels are placed in such a way that I can almost visualize the flow of energy and love between them. On the front of the table around which they are seated is a small square, an empty spot. We are invited into this empty space so that we may join the Father, Son, and Holy Spirit.

As we eat beneath this icon, we hope that our table fellowship as a family mirrors these angels' table fellowship. As we share in their table fellowship, we become part of their intimate relationship and are transformed by it.

The Trinity has fallen on hard times in many of our churches. We largely ignore it, even though it occurs again and again in our prayers, hymns, and sacramental life. It is a little like the elephant in the middle of the living room that no one mentions. References to the Trinity are everywhere, but we avoid talking about it.

Laity have been far from comfortable discussing a doctrine that seems to make even theologians stutter and stammer. Yet the doctrine of the Trinity has powerful implications for partnership, service, and leadership. The Trinity is not an abstract conceptual paradox. Neither is it a mathematical puzzle of one and three. It is instead the most practical of all doctrines.

The Trinity uses the ideas of *person* and *relationship* to affirm that God is essentially personal and relational.[9] This means that every human being has her or his origins as a person through relationship. We are persons by virtue of our relationships with God and with others. The power of being itself is ultimately relational. *This relational power is the same source that underlies all faithful leadership.*

The early interpreters of the Trinity used the Greek word *perichoresis* to describe the Trinity. *Perichoresis* means "to dance around." It is related to our English words *choreography* and *chorus.*

The three persons of the Trinity are dance partners who move in harmony with one another.

Most of us arrange the Trinity into a hierarchy. God the Creator is on top. Immediately below, we place Jesus Christ. Then, still lower, we locate the Holy Spirit. Yet the earliest church appears not to have had a hierarchical Trinity. It understood the Trinity as a dance of partnership, mutual service, and communion.

This image of Trinity provides a powerful insight into the partnership and servanthood that undergird Christian leadership. Leadership is a dance. The partners in this dance are not rigidly divided into those who lead and those who follow. These dance partners do not need to hold onto one another tightly because they move confidently in the same pattern. They do not clutch, grasp, and cling because the same music animates them. The dance of leadership has no place for the possessive clutch, the clinging arm, the heavy hand.

Dance partners can also change roles quickly and effortlessly. Now arm in arm; now face to face. Sometimes leading; sometimes following. It does not matter which since the music itself leads, not the dancers. They know that they are partners moving to the same rhythm, creating a pattern together and being invisibly sustained by it and through it.

QUESTIONS FOR REFLECTION

1. Describe some groups that do not balance advocacy with inquiry. What does it feel like to be in such a group?
2. Do you know any individuals who effectively combine being forthright with the capacity to remain open to other opinions? What, in particular, do you appreciate about these leaders? What can you learn from them about how to balance these two activities in your own life?

3. Describe some specific types of questions you would ask if you were trying to inquire effectively into other people's views? Put these phrases on a list that others can read and use.

4. Can you describe some specific types of questions or phrases you would use to advocate for your own views without alienating or offending your listeners? Put these phrases on a list that others can read and use.

5. This chapter outlines four stages of team or group development. Can you give examples of these stages from your own experience in committees and church boards?

6. Can you think of some groups that have gotten stuck in the storming stage because individuals insisted on leading with their own power rather than being a servant to the group's emerging leadership? What could you do to help these groups?

7. How does an understanding of the four stages of group development help you be a better leader and servant to the groups in which you participate?

8. This chapter uses the metaphor of a dance to describe leadership, partnership, and service. What does this metaphor illumine? What does it obscure?

9. Can you imagine another metaphor that would describe this relationship? What does this metaphor illumine? What does it obscure?

Chapter Six

Servanthood & Dealing With Differences

Building collaborative communities inevitably means dealing with differences. Only the most naive observer would suggest that church members can hammer out commonly held purposes without experiencing conflict. Christians fight with one another. Issues are personalized. Gossip obscures common sense. Powerful individuals use rules and by-laws to control debate, making political alliances more important than spirituality or reason. Moralizing judgments destroy long-standing friendships. Church fights usually explode into destructive conflict because members do not deal creatively and constructively with their differences. How we deal with our differences thus becomes a crucial question for servant leaders.

Servant leaders cannot avoid conflict. Their responsibilities often require them to go against the grain of people's expectations. Rather than providing answers, they ask questions that create dissonance. They do not shield people from new ideas that challenge their self-understanding. They instead expose these differences and allow members to address their underlying conflicts. Servant leaders do not always orient people to past roles. They instead disorient members, inviting them to try out different ways of valuing, acting, and thinking. Rather than maintain norms, servant leaders challenge existing norms and present alternative possibilities. Dealing with differences is inextricably tied to these tasks.

Most of us have a more negative view of differences. We have experienced these differences as leading to destructive conflict. Some people refuse to become church leaders because they have experienced such painful conflict. Others avoid becoming leaders because they have historically felt devalued. When differences were ranked and prioritized, powerful elites viewed these people's unique talents as unimportant.

WHAT DIFFERENCE DO OUR DIFFERENCES MAKE?

So what difference do our differences make? Are they signs of personal privilege? Do they divide us into categories such as better and worse, or superior and inferior? Or do we see our differences as diverse ways that we together serve larger, shared purposes?

Human nature seems drawn to define differences vertically. Some of us are *up*; others are *down*. Some are *superior*; others are *inferior*. Differences in ability are transformed into differences in excellence. We rank and prioritize our differences.

Christian faith proposes another perspective on our differences. We count on our differences to overcome personal limitations. We anticipate that our differences will release new resources as we collaborate. Our differences become shared strengths. Because we are not all the same, we need one another. You want to try new hymns and test out alternative styles of worship. I want to sing old, familiar gospel songs and keep the same order of worship we've always used.

We could see our differences as something to rank and prioritize: My way is better than yours. Yours is superior to mine.

This way of dealing with differences leads to conflict and win/lose situations. On the other hand, if we put our differences at each other's service, we become servant leaders who enrich and strengthen the whole community. Servanthood is the key to dealing with our differences in ways that encourage collaboration rather than conflict.

SERVANTHOOD ALLOWS US TO SEE OUR INDIVIDUAL DIFFERENCES AS COMMUNAL STRENGTHS

Dealing with differences is not new to the church. The New Testament provides ample evidence of destructive church fights over differing priorities, values, behaviors, and cultural commitments. Can the gospel be preached to the Gentiles? Must converts be circumcised? Can we eat meat sacrificed to idols? How do Christians and Jews relate to one another? These and other differences tore early congregations asunder.

MUTUAL SERVICE AS PAUL'S WAY TO DEAL WITH DIFFERENCES

Paul's letters continually address the question of how to deal with differences. The Philippians, for example, had tumbled into a nasty church fight. In Paul's letter to them, he reminds them of a better way: Do nothing from selfish ambition. Do not be conceited. Do not look to your own interests, but be willing to serve your opponents' interests (Philippians 2:3-4). He argues that partnerships in the gospel depend not on the assertion of one's own rights but on relating to the other person's needs instead. Taking the perspective of a servant, according to Paul, allows us to see our differences as a shared strength rather than as a personal threat.

Like Jesus, the Philippians should not be concerned only with their own interests. Paul invites them to instead empty themselves in mutual service to one another. For Jesus did not count equality with God something to be exploited. He instead emptied himself and became a servant (Philippians 2:6-11). We deal with our differences creatively and constructively when we become servants to one another. Our differences become shared strengths when we regard one another from the perspective of mutual service.

Paul, in arguing that servanthood is the single most important value for dealing with our differences, is not alone in the New Testament.

MATTHEW'S GOSPEL: A MANUAL ON DEALING WITH DIFFERENCES

Of the Gospels, Matthew's in particular assumes a mixed community characterized by differences and conflict. Matthew seems to have written from the perspective of an ethnically diverse community of Jewish and Gentile Christians. While Gentiles are prominent in his Gospel, he also refers positively to scribes and Pharisees. Matthew includes the Great Commandment to go and make disciples of all nations (Matthew 28:19). He records how the Roman centurion at Capernaum had greater faith than anyone in Israel (8:10). Gentile magi come bearing gifts for the Christ Child, whose parents are portrayed as humble Jews (1:18–2:12). Jesus comes to fulfill the Torah, not to abolish it (5:17). And even the scribes are portrayed in a positive light (13:52).

Matthew's community consists of rich and poor as well as Greek and Jew. Luke writes of small coins and copper currency. Matthew speaks of silver and gold. Matthew blesses the poor in spirit and those who hunger and thirst for righteousness, modifying Luke's more stringent Beatitudes.

Matthew tells the parable of the weeds that grow amid the wheat (Matthew 13:24-30, 36-43). His community does not consist of the pure and pious. It is a mixed community of rich and poor, Jew and Greek, faithful and fallen. Indeed, Matthew introduces the term *church* (*ecclesia*) precisely to describe this mixed community of saints and sinners (18:17).

Matthew's diverse community clearly experienced conflict between its members, so Matthew was particularly interested in how Jesus dealt with differences. Matthew offers one of the most profound and remarkable treatments of power and leadership in the New Testament.

Matthew 18 begins with a question about status and power: "Who is the greatest in the kingdom of heaven?" (verse 1). Jesus responds by drawing attention to a child, "Whoever becomes humble like this child is the greatest in the kingdom of heaven" (verse 4). Whenever people have different gifts, we are tempted to prioritize our abilities. Some are superior. Others are inferior. The great ones possess important talents and abilities. The little ones have gifts of marginal importance. In drawing attention to a child, Jesus diminishes this tendency to rank our differences into superior and inferior categories.

Jesus then admonishes his disciples to see themselves as servants to the little ones whom powerful elites routinely devalue. Because they are different from the powerful and well-placed, the world's little ones are easily discounted. Greatness in God's reign, however, belongs to those who reach across the stumbling block of differences and serve God's little ones. "If any of you put a stumbling block before one of these little ones who believe in me, it would be better for you if a great millstone were fastened around your neck and you were drowned in the depth of the sea" (Matthew 18:6).

Matthew next turns to issues of scandal and offense. Wherever people are different, one person will be scandalized by another's behavior. Other people are not doing things "the way we've always done it." Matthew's response is to remind his readers to "take care that you do not despise one of these little ones" (Matthew 18:10). Do not look down on those who are different, Jesus admonishes. We treat them as little ones, not worth our time and energy. Such contempt for those who are different does not build up the body of Christ; it fractures and divides the community of faith. Faithful Christian leaders are characterized by humble service, not by contemptuous domination.

Finally, Matthew shows keen insight into how people deal with differences and address conflict. Many of us deal with differences by "triangulating" others. That is, rather than face our differences head on, we go around the person with whom we disagree and appeal to a higher authority.

Sarah is upset about how Ben is chairing the long-range planning committee. Rather than speaking to Ben about the problem, Sarah goes to the pastor and asks him to do something about Ben's behavior.

The Berea Bible Class is upset with their pastor's preaching. They do not make an appointment and talk to their preacher about their concerns. Instead they call the district superintendent and complain about their preacher.

In Matthew 18:15-17, Jesus tells his disciples that they are to deal directly with their differences. They are not to "triangulate" others. They are to go personally to the one with whom they disagree and talk through their differences. They are not to go over their opponent's head to a higher authority until they have first tried to work through the conflict on their own. Furthermore, they may not approach their opponent as an inferior whom they are correcting. They are to go in humility, as servants who seek to restore the broken body of Christ to wholeness.

> If another member of the church sins against you, go
> and point out the fault when the two of you are alone.
> If the member listens to you, you have regained that
> one. But if you are not listened to, take one or two oth-
> ers along with you, so that every word may be con-
> firmed by the evidence of two or three witnesses. If the
> member refuses to listen to them, tell it to the church;
> and if the offender refuses to listen even to the church,
> let such a one be to you as a Gentile and a tax collec-
> tor. (Matthew 18:15-17)

Usually, we would interpret "let [the offender] be to you as a Gentile and a tax collector" to mean that we can dismiss and exclude the person. Yet this is not Matthew's usual attitude toward tax collectors and Gentiles. They are precisely the people we seek out, welcome, and include. These are the ones we serve even as Jesus the Servant sought them out and invited them to sit at God's banquet table. Matthew's final chapter has Jesus instructing his disciples to go out to the Gentiles and invite them into the Kingdom (Matthew 28:19).

Conflict and differences are not to be avoided. In embracing our differences, we discover a deeper communion that lies beneath our differences. One of the most pervasive differences that church members must embrace is the gender difference. Men and women work side by side on church boards and committees. Yet many times they do not become partners and collaborators, engaged in mutual service to God and one another. Reflecting on how we deal with these differences provides us with clues for handling other differences in the church.

MEN, WOMEN, AND LEADERSHIP

Some researchers have suggested that women and men are socialized into different cultures as children.[10] As a result, they learn different "languages" through which they communicate with others. These differences in culture and communication create opportunities for misunderstanding and conflict.

The idea of two cultures has intuitive appeal because it confirms our stereotypes of men and women. Yet some researchers are now proposing that status and power differences sometimes hide behind what seem to be gender differences. These differences are not really about gender but about power and status. When women are in high status roles, they tend to adopt instrumental communication styles that focus on teaching practical goals and solving problems. They also exhibit more dominant behaviors. Conversely, men in low status roles reflect more expressive communication styles that express feelings and establish rapport. If this is true, dealing with gender differences in the church is really a way of addressing the more fundamental differences of power and status among us, regardless of gender.

A TALE OF TWO CULTURES

Boys traditionally play in large groups, usually outdoors, and farther away from home than girls do, these researchers suggest. Boys are therefore under less adult scrutiny and are more likely to act independently. Boys' groups are also more often hierarchically organized. They achieve status in groups through dominant behaviors such as telling others what to do. Boys' games usually have winners and losers, encouraging a culture of dominance and power. Girls, on the other hand, are perceived to traditionally play in groups nearer home. Their games are less likely to have winners and losers. As a result, their culture places a higher value on cooperation and relationships.

DIFFERENT STYLES OF COMMUNICATION

While not true of all men and women, there is evidence that men are more likely to use instrumental communication styles. Women, on the other hand, rely on expressive communication. An instrumental style focuses on reaching practical goals and finding solutions to problems. An expressive style values the expression of feelings and sensitivity to others.

Differences in communication styles can result in a mismatch between expectations and reality. An individual reveals a problem and expects understanding. The listener, however, understands this as an invitation to propose solutions. Rather than receiving sympathy, the individual receives advice. When such a mismatch occurs, people feel confused and frustrated. Sometimes they are hurt and angry.

Another gender difference has been described as the conflict between *rapport talk* and *report talk*. Some people—usually women—communicate to establish rapport. They use communication to establish and strengthen relationships. Other people—usually men—talk to exhibit knowledge or skills. Women's conversations frequently involve personal sharing about what is happening in their lives. They also talk about other people. This talking about others does not necessarily connote destructive or negative comments; rather, it entails attention to people and their lives. Men, on the other hand, prefer to exchange impersonal information about events in the world of politics, sports, economics, or the weather. Both styles carry liabilities for men and women. Impersonal conversation does not open men up in the same way that personal sharing does. On the other hand, women can appear unknowledgeable about the world of work and society.

Those who study gender differences in communication suggest that both men and women would be better served if they appreciated these differences and learned to embrace each other's communication styles. Some men may need to learn the value of appropriate personal self-disclosure. Some women may benefit from talking more about impersonal topics.

SERVANTHOOD AND DEALING WITH OUR DIFFERENCES

We sometimes try to deal with these differences by seeing them as deficits: Some ways of communicating are better than others. Some ways of acting are superior to others. This approach ultimately leads to destructive conflict. Nothing hurts worse than to be told that your intentions are bad when you know that they are good. Nothing wounds us more than being told we are doing something wrong when we are merely doing it our own way.

When we see ourselves as servants, however, we perceive our differences as strengths. I serve you by creating a hospitable and open space where you are valued and free to share your gifts. You feel empowered by my service. Out of your new-found strength, you reach out in service to me, inviting me to share my gifts. Servant leaders release a continuous cycle of service when they treat differences as strengths to be shared rather than as deficits to be corrected.

THE DANGERS OF SERVANTHOOD AS A MODEL FOR LEADERS

As we reflect on these differences between women and men, we also realize that we need to be careful in applying the image of servant. Too frequently this image has reinforced women's traditional roles and relationships. Rather than liberating them, this image has oppressed them. Those who are already powerless do not need to be told to give up power. Women's capacity to lead with power needs to be affirmed and set within a larger framework of service, mutuality, and collaboration. Otherwise, servanthood reinforces traditional stereotypes of women's roles in church and society.

HANDLING CONFLICT

Learning to collaborate across these differences in status and power requires that we rethink our perspective on conflict. When we rank and prioritize our differences, destructive conflict is almost inevitable. Seeing our differences as strengths, on the other hand, creates opportunities for creative conflict that deepens our partnerships, strengthens our mutual service, and empowers our mission.

As a leader, how do you react to conflict? Most people have a particular personal style in dealing with conflict. Five typical responses to conflict are avoidance, accommodation, domination, compromise, and integration.[11] We can plot these on a grid that has as one axis the importance of the relationship with our opponent, and as the other axis the importance of our personal goals (see Figure 3).

Figure 3

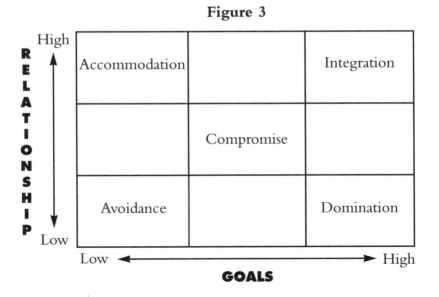

AVOIDANCE

Some leaders simply do not like to admit that conflict exists. They operate under the unrealistic hope that if they ignore the conflict, it will go away. They blame conflict on "outside agitators." They change the subject when someone mentions a controversial topic. Leaders who avoid conflict neither value their partnership with others nor have strong purposes that guide them. If they did, they would not avoid conflict. They would not hide in their shell like a turtle.

The difficulty with this approach is that most conflicts do not go away. They can be delayed or temporarily ignored, but this is not the same as resolving the underlying issue. Leaders who avoid conflict are not serving their communities; they are only allowing their communities to postpone inevitable conflicts. Often, because the conflict has been repressed, the underlying problems continue to fester and spread. Then when conflict finally erupts, it is more destructive than it would otherwise have been.

ACCOMMODATION

Like the avoider, the accommodator feels uncomfortable with conflict. Instead of ignoring differences and disagreements, however, this leader brings the conflict to a quick end by giving in easily. If the avoider is a turtle, the accommodator is a teddy bear, wanting to be liked and admired. Leaders who too easily accommodate are often insecure. They are overly worried about acceptance and approval. The importance of relationships is so high that the accommodating leader is willing to sacrifice goals and purposes.

Accommodation is a poor way to deal with conflict. It does not generate creative thinking about the issue. More important, the accommodator eventually comes to resent caving in too easily. These feelings of resentment fuel the fires of future conflicts. Congregations are not well served by leaders who prefer accommodation as a way to deal with conflict. Issues seem to be resolved, but the underlying conflict is never addressed and the process of accommodation itself produces new resentment and hostility.

DOMINATION

The dominator is like a Sherman tank. He turns every difference into a win/lose situation. The leader with this conflict style can be aggressive, willing to use threats and coercion to force others into submission.

Relationships mean nothing to the dominating leader. All that matters are his personal goals and purposes. Moreover, this style is likely to generate post-conflict tension, resentment, and hostility. Differences are really never settled. They are instead made worse.

COMPROMISE

Our culture tends to view compromise as the best way to deal with differences. You give a little. I give a little. We meet in the middle. Everyone goes away with something.

Unfortunately, compromise can be as destructive to congregations as any of our earlier conflict styles. Rather than partners engaged in mutual service among equals, it creates individuals seeking their own maximum satisfaction. In order to gain a tactical advantage in the negotiation, one person may be tempted to misrepresent and manipulate others.

INTEGRATION

While compromise entails splitting the difference between positions, integration involves a sincere effort to find new solutions that maximize everyone's satisfaction. Participants highly value their mutual relationship. They embrace collaboration. At the same time, they are strongly motivated by shared purposes and goals. This combination of shared purposes and collaborative partnerships gives rise to a spirit of servanthood. Participants seek to serve one another and the larger purposes that unite them by generating new solutions and innovative approaches.

Instead of leaving a post-conflict residue of resentment, hostility, or frustration, integrating leaders produce a climate of respect and trust. This trust becomes the foundation for mutual service and collaboration.

The following guidelines may help foster integrative approaches to conflict:

• Make communication honest and open. Do not withhold information or misrepresent your position. Avoid deceit and manipulation.

• Phrase your statements about the other person's position in specific terms rather than global ones. Global comments are more easily taken as personal insults. For example, avoid statements that begin, "You always . . ." Even if you disagree with your opponent, do not make him or her wrong.

• Assume responsibility for your own feelings and preferences. Do not say, "You make me mad." Instead say, "I feel angry when you . . ." Then state precisely what new actions or behaviors you would like to see. People cannot change who they are. They can change what they do.

• Put a great deal of effort into clarifying your respective positions. Everyone needs to understand precisely where the disagreement between them lies.

• Communicate your flexibility and willingness to modify your position.

• Emphasize your underlying partnership rather than what

divides and separates you. Focus on the larger shared interests that unite you rather than on the specific positions over which you disagree.

Matthew ends this section of his Gospel (18:1-22) with a question from Peter: "Lord, if another member of the church sins against me, how often should I forgive? As many as seven times?" Jesus' answer is revealing. He says, "Not seven times, but, I tell you, seventy-seven times" (Matthew 18:21-22). He then follows this with a parable about a servant. This servant receives a totally gracious forgiveness of his debt but then refuses to forgive the debt of a fellow servant (18:23-35). The connection between servanthood, forgiveness, and partnerships in the Gospel is unavoidable.

Forgiving seventy-seven times is going beyond the expected. Most of us use baseball rules: three strikes and you're out. But Jesus insists on an unbelievable level of forgiveness in church life. There is a wise lesson in this. I have hardly ever met anyone who left the church because it was too forgiving. Yet I have encountered many people who reject the church because of its harsh judgments against those who are labeled as different. Dealing with differences entails the capacity to forgive. Like servants who have been forgiven much, we should be generous in our judgment of those whose differences offend us. Only in such a climate of forgiveness can mutual service become a catalyst for collaborative partnerships in the gospel.

QUESTIONS FOR REFLECTION

1. Matthew 18 suggests that when we differ with a brother or sister in Christ, we should go directly to him or her rather than pull rank and go to his or her superior. Can you think of some examples of church members "triangulating" others by drawing them into a conflict? Can you describe some

situations in which people successfully followed the advice in Matthew 18?

2. How do you view conflict? Do you fear it? Do you see it as a potentially positive dynamic? What is your initial reaction to conflict with another person? As a leader, what is your reaction when you must address a conflict between others?

3. How do you view differences between people? Are they something to rank and prioritize? Do they mutually enhance one another? What difference does it make in your work as a leader?

4. What do you think about differences between men and women? Does the research on differences such as *report talk* and *rapport talk*, talking about *things* and talking about *people*, expecting *problem-solving* and expecting *understanding*, explain dynamics you have seen between men and women on committees or church boards? In what ways?

5. What is your reaction to the observation that an emphasis on servanthood can disempower women or people who have traditionally been kept in subservient positions? How is this possible? What are the ways we can use the language of servanthood without disempowering some people?

6. Can you give examples of how conflicts have been poorly handled by avoiders, accommodators, dominators, and compromisers? What could have been done differently in those situations? How could an emphasis on servanthood have made a difference?

7. The text gives several guidelines for collaborative responses to conflict. How might these be helpful to you? Can you think of additional guidelines that the author has overlooked?

Conclusion

Among You As One Who Serves

Servant leaders make power more abundant. They lead in ways that strengthen others rather than render them dependent. Servant leaders leave others more creative, imaginative, and forward-thinking than they were before.

Servant leaders are less interested in the exercise of power itself than in the empowerment of others. They lead by inspiring rather than ordering, by freeing people to use their own initiative and experiences rather than by denying others or constraining their actions. They seek responsibility and interconnection rather than authority and autonomy.

Servant leaders understand that they participate in leadership but do not possess it. Leadership is ultimately a relationship of mutual influence between partners in the gospel who intend real changes that reflect common purposes.

> The greatest among you must become like the youngest, and the leader like one who serves. For who is greater, the one who is at the table or the one who serves? Is it not the one at the table? But I am among you as one who serves. (Luke 22:26–27)

For Further Reading

As One With Authority: Reflective Leadership in Ministry, by Jackson Carroll (Westminster John Knox Press, 1991). Carroll's book argues that we have failed to take seriously the important function of authority in church organizations. Written primarily for pastors, Carroll examines the nature of authority and defines key functions that leaders perform.

Getting to Yes: Negotiating Agreement Without Giving In, by Roger Fisher and William Ury (Penguin USA, 1991). Fisher and Ury's work is based on their research with the Harvard Negotiation Project. It provides helpful and concrete advice for negotiating differences and handling conflicts.

God for Us: The Trinity and Christian Life, by Catherine Mowry Lacugna (HarperSanFrancisco, 1991). This book emphasizes the relational nature of Christian life and the importance of partnership. The Christian life rests upon the foundation of relationship and partnership because it emerges from the Trinity, which itself expresses a relational, dynamic partnership.

*Growing in Authority, Relinquishing Control: A New Approach to
Leadership*, by Celia Allison Hahn (The Alban Institute,
1994). Hahn's book explores the relationship between
authority, power, and control. Her book provides an especially helpful perspective on gender differences as they relate
to power and authority.

*Servant Leadership: A Journey Into the Nature of Legitimate Power
and Greatness*, by Robert Greenleaf (Paulist Press, 1983).
Greenleaf's book is a basic resource on servant leadership.
Greenleaf coined and popularized the concept of servant
leadership in this book.

The Learning Congregation: A New Vision of Leadership, by
Thomas R. Hawkins (Westminster John Knox Press, 1997).
Hawkins explores the relationship between leadership and
learning at individual, team, and congregational levels. The
chapters on team learning contain useful information about
collaborative environments, shared spaces, and principles of
group development.

Endnotes

1. For a full discussion of power, see *Power: The Inner Experience*, by David McClelland (Irvington, 1975). McClelland uses a four-fold typology of receiving, autonomous, assertive, and integrative power. I have reduced this to a three-fold typology that equates autonomous power with *power-within*, assertive power with *power-over*, and integrative power with *power-with*. Also see *PastorPower*, by Martha E. Stortz (Abingdon Press, 1993) for a three-fold typology of power based on *power-over*, *power-within*, and *power-with*.

2. For a careful examination of how the words *leadership*, *leader*, and *lead* have been used historically, see *Leadership for the Twenty-First Century*, by Joseph Rost (Praeger, 1991). Rost emphasizes the relational nature of leadership. His work builds on the important work of James MacGregor Burns. See Burns's *Leadership* (HarperCollins, 1985).

3. For a discussion of social practices, see *After Virtue: A Study in Moral Theory*, by Alasdair MacIntyre (University of Notre Dame Press, 1984). A recent book that examines Christian practices is *Practicing Our Faith: A Way of Life for a Searching People*, Dorothy Bass, editor (Jossey-Bass Publishers, 1997).

4. Raymond Brown's commentaries on John's Gospel and the Johannine Epistles form the basis for much of this chapter. See his *The Epistles of John*, Anchor Bible, volume 30 (Doubleday, 1982), and *The Gospel According to John*, Anchor Bible, volume 29 (Doubleday, 1970).

5. For a theological perspective on partnership, see *The Future of Partnership*, by Letty Russell (Westminster John Knox Press, 1979). Russell's *Church in the Round: Feminist Interpretation of the Church* (Westminster John Knox Press, 1993) also provides useful insights into the nature of partnership as a theological concept.

6. For more information about shared spaces, see Eric Eisenberg and H. L. Goodall's *Organizational Communication: Balancing Creativity and Constraint* (St. Martin's Press, 2nd edition 1997). The following description of shared spaces owes much to this book and a discussion of its ideas among myself and several other graduate students at the University of Illinois/Urbana-Champaign.

7. For further information about balancing advocacy and inquiry, see *Theory in Practice: Increasing Professional Effectiveness*, by Chris Argyris and Donald Schon (Jossey-Bass Publishers, 1992).

8. This standard categorization of group stages will be familiar to most individuals who have participated in small-group experiences. They are part of the common vocabulary of many consultants on group dynamics. A more formal discussion of these stages and their strengths and limitations can be found in *Decision-Making Group Interaction*, by Bobby

Patton, Kim Giffin, and Eleanor N. Patton (HarperCollins, 1989), pages 58–67.

9. For a perspective on theological interpretation of the Trinity, see *Trinity and Society*, by Leonardo Boff, Theology and Liberation Series (Orbis Books, 1988). Catherine Mowry Lacugna's *God For Us: The Trinity and Christian Life* (HarperSanFrancisco, 1993) provides a helpful perspective on partnership as a consequence of trinitarian thinking.

10. For gender differences in communication, see *You Just Don't Understand: Women and Men in Conversation*, by Deborah Tannen (Ballantine Books, 1990).

11. Many church consultants who specialize in conflict management, as well as many pastors, will be familiar with these five styles. A more formal discussion can be found in *Communicating for Results: A Guide for Business and the Professions*, by Cheryl Hamilton with Cordell Parker (Wadsworth Publishing Company, 1993).